Harry Golden

SO WHAT ELSE IS NEW?

By Harry Golden

ONLY IN AMERICA

FOR 2¢ PLAIN

ENJOY, ENJOY!

CARL SANDBURG

YOU'RE ENTITLE'

FORGOTTEN PIONEER

MR. KENNEDY AND THE NEGROES

SO WHAT ELSE IS NEW?

HARRY GOLDEN

So What Else

Is New?

AUTHOR OF *Only In America*

NEW YORK

G. P. PUTNAM'S SONS

Second Impression

Library of Congress Catalog Card Number: 64-21154

PRINTED IN THE UNITED STATES OF AMERICA

To Adlai E. Stevenson

Table of Contents

CONTENTS

CONTENTS

CONTENTS

CONTENTS

CONTENTS

Introduction

I sent this, my eighth book, off to my publishers the day after President Lyndon Johnson signed the Civil Rights Act of 1964 which a little over a year before, John F. Kennedy had sent to the Congress.

When I first came South some twenty-odd years ago, Negroes still stepped off the sidewalk as the white approached. As late as 1942 I saw Negroes in the South tip their hats to strange white men who passed them on the street. This is all gone, even in the State of Mississippi. That is how much life has changed for all of us.

In addition, my own life changed after I wrote my first book. In the days before *Only in America,* I used to write the whole of the *Carolina Israelite,* my personal journal; I read all proofs myself, pasted it up and delivered it to the post office when it was printed. Beside my desk I kept a barrel into which I tossed scraps of paper with scribblings. Each of these was a lead sentence for an essay. When the paper came due, I would spend two or three days and nights at the desk, dipping into the barrel and presto! I had the whole paper of twenty pages, tabloid size, ready for the printer. The rest of the month I spent selling advertising space, answering mail, and discussing with my secretary, war and peace, love and life, and we used to wonder together whether we would accumulate enough money in the petty cash to pay the telephone bill.

But literary fame lured me not only onto television but out along the lecture circuit. The first thing to go was the barrel. Where once there was only a desk, a lamp, a portable typewriter, now there are four desks all lit by heavy neons, an IBM electric, and in place of the barrel are several rows of steel files. Writing a syndicated column three times a week, lecturing sixty times a year, writing a book every eighteen months and occasional articles for national magazines means no more discussions with the secretary about war and peace or worrying about the telephone bills. In fact, our personal discussions now center upon the secretary's fringe and retirement benefits, which is as it should be.

But as I noted, momentous changes overtook all of us—so I would have changed anyway. What interests me more, however, is the significant changes in the attitudes of people around me. "Harry," says a fellow I meet on the street, "I suppose you don't know me any more." As a matter of fact, I didn't know him in the first place. Or a lady calls and says her son, home from college, would like to meet me and can I come to dinner Friday night. Well, no I can't come to dinner Friday night. I have never been to dinner there before and see no pressing reason why I should start Friday. But up in Leo's Delicatessen, said lady bitterly complains, "He's a big shot now, won't come to dinner any more." "Any more" are the key words. She has succeeded in making a non-existent friendship and a first dinner invitation retroactive.

These are minor annoyances. The Ku Kluxers who telephone me in the early hours of the morning are also minor annoyances. One tolerates them. One has no choice. The real satisfaction comes from plain, decent Southerners (by the thousand) who are not inviting me to dinner but writing me to say, "I work for a large insurance company in Mobile and it wouldn't do for me to say anything openly but my wife and I agree with you on the race issue and hope the country can find a solution soon." It comes from a note from Dr. Martin Luther King who says, "Your writings have been an inspiration." It comes when other writers tell me my last book was a good one. And it comes from the knowledge that over a half million people have written me personal letters during these past years at the rate of about a thousand a week. The Jewish housewife writes that I remind her of her uncle when she was a child; the Gentile mother writes that her early life in Boston, or in Minnesota was not much different from mine on New York's Lower East Side.

My one ambition was that if I could ever afford it, I would have the barber come to my office and I would have a fellow to drive me because I hate to drive and can never find my way around unless I go to the Post Office and start from there. These I have achieved. And every other year I can visit London and Jerusalem. You will see I do not tremble at the charge of "dual allegiance." In fact, I am a triple allegiance man—America, England, and Israel, the last two in alphabetical order.

HARRY GOLDEN

July 4, 1964
Charlotte, North Carolina

Harry Golden, Jr., the editor

SOME YEARS ago, before he won the Pulitzer Prize for his editorials about the racial crisis in Little Rock, Arkansas, Harry Ashmore was the editor of the Charlotte *News*. One afternoon, Ashmore said to me, "Harry, you will never produce a book on your own because you have no interior discipline. Why don't you ask your son, Harry Jr., to edit your writings into a book?"

Harry, Jr. was then City Hall and police reporter for the Charlotte *Observer* (nowadays he is feature writer and rewrite man for the Detroit *Free Press*). Ask him to edit my writings is just what I did. The result was *Only in America*. Since then, Harry, Jr. has edited, collated, corrected spelling and syntax, written new heads and chapter titles for four successive books, including this one. This is my first chance to thank him publicly. I am glad I knew a Harry Ashmore to put me straight. I am even happier I had a Harry, Jr.

PART 1

America and the Evil Eye

Repartee

In CHARLOTTE not too long ago, a civic group convened to try to discuss the problem of juvenile delinquency. One of the speakers was particularly concerned about perversion and during the course of his remarks, he leaned over the table and asked a colleague, "What do you call a man who loves another man?"

One of the ladies on the committee immediately spoke up. "A Christian," she said.

So what else is new?

The BEATLE HAIRCUT was the height of fashion in medieval times. The young minstrels and troubadours with Beatle haircuts went all over Europe and the ladies swooned with delight as the troubadours sang, "I want to hold your hand, I want to be your man." So what else is new?

Point of information

The BOYS who ran in and out of the pushcarts in the Jewish casbah of New York City still wrote most of America's popular songs—"Waitin' for the Robert E. Lee," "Carolina Moon," "Swanee," "Alabam'," and a few thousand others. Forty years after Wolfie Gilbert wrote "Waitin' for the Robert E. Lee," he penned a letter to me in which he asked, "Harry,

now that you're down South, would you please let me know
what is a levee?"

John Steinbeck's Okies

WHERE ARE the Joads of *The Grapes of Wrath?*
Thirty years after California met the dusted-out Okies
with armed guards on her borders, those who came in anyway look back on those first years as mighty slim pickings.
They had a love of owning land and most of them eventually
got a-holt of a few acres. A subdivision grew here and there
and some of the Okies woke up to find their land had made
them rich. Others opened service stations, car repair shops,
some of their women opened beauty shops, trained in hospitals to be nurses' aides, sent their children through high school
and college and now the third generation has produced teachers, engineers and physicians.
Remember what Ma Joad said: "We are the people."

Mitch Miller's men

I LOVE *Sing Along with Mitch.* I like to watch all those
big homely fat guys as well as the short homely guys singing for
all they're worth. It reminds me of the old days among the
union organizers and the radicals.
You'll notice the American Medical Association and the
National Association of Manufacturers do not sing.
In the early days of the New Deal we all sang the TVA*
song (to the tune of "On Top of Old Smokey"):

* TVA—Tennessee Valley Administration.

> Where once private power
> Said it couldn't be done
> You can see farmlights twinkling,
> You can hear high lines hum.
> Fertilizer and power
> are reclaiming the soil
> And REA* co-ops help
> lighten the toil.

But the few conservatives on the Lower East Side of New York were rather cynical about the whole thing (to the tune of *Maryland, My Maryland*):

> The working class can kiss my ass,
> I got the foreman's job at last.

Winner by a mule

LYNDON B. JOHNSON, who was criticized for lifting his beagles by their ears, will somehow solve the problem of the dogs. Democrats have always realized the public relations value of animals. I am still convinced that President Harry Truman pulled off his unexpected victory of 1948 because of a mule.

President Truman won because he carried four of the farm states which even Franklin D. Roosevelt had lost in 1944. On one of his whistle stops through Kansas, Mr. Truman and some of his aides walked down the road a piece to shake hands with some of the local farmers. One farmer, standing beside his

* REA—Rural Electrification Administration.

mule, asked, "Mr. President, I heard tell you followed the
plow. Now you tell me how old this mule is." With the newsreel cameras grinding away, Mr. Truman opened the mule's
mouth, searched it a minute, and said, "Eight years and six
months."

The old farmer went hysterical with joy. "You're right," he
shouted, and then and there Harry Truman picked up three
million farm votes and beat the city feller, Thomas E. Dewey.

Charcoal steaks

I HAVE begun to wonder about my fellow man. It seems
that we are going primitive again. The other afternoon I flew,
in a beautifully clear afternoon, back to my home base of
Charlotte and found a thick blue haze over the city.

Then I realized what was going on below. It was Saturday
afternoon—and the outdoor chefs were at it again.

We've spent centuries getting cooking inside, removing the
smoke from the ceiling, finally coming up with electric cooking, and now experimenting with all kinds of quick, painless
indoor cooking. But, all of a sudden, there is the great urge to
go outside again.

Everyone has an outdoor grill. Not only in sprawling urban
centers like Charlotte where the masses flee to the suburbs, but
in places like New York City and Detroit, too.

You go to the Sears Store, buy an outdoor grill, pick up a bag
of charcoal and some lighter fluid, and take your food outside
and cook it. After it is cooked, you flee from the flies and bugs
and take it inside to eat.

I have done some research on this, and I find the food
usually is very unsatisfactory. First of all, it doesn't taste like

charcoal or have a charcoal flavor. That is supposed to be the reason for it. Secondly, it tastes a bit like the lighter, or "starter" as they call it.

One friend tells me that you sprinkle charcoal flavoring on top of the meat to give it an additional taste of charcoal. That would be charcoal over charcoal. He added that he likes to use a "tenderizer," too. All these added ingredients give the meat a new flavor, but I doubt if it is a meat flavor.

Beef is beef to me. Let it alone. All you need is heat.

"One other thing," the friend told me. "Cooking outside entertains the kids."

That must be the reason.

Some notes in passing

BARRY GOLDWATER? I always knew the first Jewish President of the United States would be an Episcopalian.

This retirement at sixty-five, so arbitrary an age, is an American tragedy. I believe it has been foisted on all of us by the insurance companies and their silly actuarial tables.

One of the nice things to have in this world would be a marital guarantee, making a marriage good for five years say, or for ten or for thirty.

To me, as a layman, the most impressive thing about Judaism is that Moses did not become a god. That the Hebrews did not make a god out of Moses is perhaps the most civilizing idea in the entire history of theology.

The comic strip is the lowest common denominator of art—it is the one artistic endeavor that people who read only the newspapers can understand. Television is an animated comic strip. It is art for people who don't even read the newspapers.

The Israeli Prime Minister Eshkol has sent an ultimatum to Castro. Mr. Eshkol said, "An attack on Miami will be considered an attack on Israel."

In 1964, I listened to a speech by Republican Governor Romney of Michigan. I shut my eyes and for a moment he sounded for all the world like Henry A. Wallace in his third party race for President in 1948.

We are a child-oriented culture because once upon a time there was a reason for such an orientation. The teen-agers control the country's habits and markets because we are an immigrant culture, a culture in which the kids told their parents and grandparents how to talk, dress, and conduct themselves in the open society.

Self-esteem

A MAN needs recognition by the world. A woman, however, needs recognition by only a few persons, but that recognition is vital. A woman will take steps to get this if it is denied her and will make sure she is noticed one way or another.

My advice to men is to send every woman they know two dozen red roses or a like token at proper intervals. That way her fierce loyalty will be fanned to white heat and everything will go along smoothly.

Rapid reading

WHAT do rapid readers read?

They read clichés.

The trick with a book, a newspaper, a magazine, a business report, or even a stock market prospectus is to get what is inside the covers out—without the bother of turning all those pages. Since no one has mastered this trick as yet, or at any rate mastered it to any great degree, most people are consigned to the tedium of page turning.

Along came the rapid readers with the promise that they had a method where you could virtually flip the pages, as though you were watching a movie.

In other words, you can read passively instead of actively.

But this is obviously not reading, any more than going to the movies or watching television can be called learning. No lawyer who has prepared an important brief wants a rapid-reading judge nor have I noticed since the proliferation of rapid-reading teachers that there has been any noticeable improvement in understanding the income tax forms.

Much of this thinking has been inspired by Professor Reuben Brower of Harvard, who has contributed an article to a recent issue of *Daedalus*, in which he says the rapid-reading vogue, which he calls book reading, represents "the American passion for quick and easy solutions, the importance attached by parents and teachers to high scores in tests necessary for admission to college," and the like.

The rapid-reading teachers are the ones who have corrupted

our language with such concepts as "language skills," "reading skills," "recognition skills," "content fields," and "content analysis," and "language immaturities." A climactic sentence in one of these reports about rapid reading, says Professor Brower, ends with: "the desired pupil learning outcomes."

You would have to read this rapidly simply to put up with it.

The real secret to rapid reading is precisely this: if it doesn't interest you, you don't read it at all.

America and the evil eye

SOME years ago I passed on my favorite recipe for avoiding the Evil Eye. The Evil Eye is always on the lookout for the successful, the healthy, or the happy. So when someone congratulated me on any good fortune, I would look sad and reply: "Yes, but my teeth are killing me. I don't know what I will do—probably may have to have all of them pulled without anesthetic." This reduced resentment on the part of "the public" and led the Evil Eye astray. He looked for greener pastures. He is after a guy whose day and prospects are absolutely bright, not a fellow about to lose his choppers.

Dr. Irma Drooz, a subscriber, remembered this recipe and it prompted her to send me a clipping from the A.M.A. News. Dr. James Watson, who, along with two British scientists, won the Nobel Prize for his role in discovering the molecular structure of dioxyribonucleic acid, told reporters: "It is an important thing we have accomplished, but we have not done away with the common cold—which I now have."

And the Evil Eye snapped his fingers in dismay. There was no point in bothering the good doctor. The doctor knows how to ward off the Evil Eye. He is one of us and I hope my strategy had something to do with it.

Some of my friends and readers express great shock at my belief in the Evil Eye. "You," they say, "of all people . . . *you!* Superstitious!" But childhood memory is deep and my mother was such a complete believer in the Evil Eye that I just can't shake the fear off.

"It's bad when things are too good" worries me, which is why I welcome critical pieces or editorial blasts against me. I save these pieces and guard them with my life. The Evil Eye sees this and says, "Well, he ain't got it so good," and leaves me alone.

Why are so many people unhappy in America today? Is it drive for status? Is it high taxes? Neither. If you will spit three times and turn an empty glass upside down, knock wood, and make a fig with your thumb between two forefingers, I'll tell you. It's the Evil Eye makes them sad. As mother said, "It's bad when things are too good." The people feel things are too good and something must happen to spoil life.

People appreciate compliments but on the other hand, like my mother, they are frightened of hearing them. When you compliment a woman she will invariably say, "I'm just an old hag," or, "My hair is terrible," or, "I've learned how to hide the wrinkles." All of which is calculated to ward off the Evil Eye.

We must not rule out a sense of guilt concerning our happiness. How can we actually enjoy this tremendous American opulence when children are starving throughout the world? How can we be happy when millions are in misery? And unfortunately, millions of people cannot be helped by knocking on wood or spitting three times. It takes sacrifice. Our willingness to understand that a fleet is as fast as its slowest ship

teaches us somehow that it cannot remain good forever while
there is disease, misery, poverty, elsewhere.

Sex

LIFE offers us many joys and ecstasies. There is the
anticipation just as the velvet curtain rises to reveal the stage,
the novelty of the trip abroad, the enthusiasm of getting your
first job. In friendship there is great comfort, and great pride in
becoming a grandfather. Perhaps none of these is comparable
with sex, but the degree of difference between all of them and
sex is not that great. What makes sex the paramount goal is
not necessarily pleasure, joy, or satisfaction, *but the instinct for
life.* Sex is the one activity furthest removed from the shadow
of death. Life presents no better affirmation of itself than sex.
That is why sex will always remain the supremely gratifying
goal of life.

Frau Haydn and the Soviet

THE GREAT German composer Haydn had slept in the
snow and starved and endured severe distress for his music. He
became famous and rich and he married. Frau Haydn took her
husband seriously. She was younger than he was and she
wanted to be sure that after his death she would be able to
perpetuate his memory properly. So she built herself a big
house to which she would retire when widowed. One wing
of the house was a museum where all of her husband's compositions would be stored and where the eager public could

read books about him. But what happened was that Frau Haydn died first. The joke, more or less, was on her.

Frau Haydn reminds me of the Soviet Union. The hopes of both Stalin and Khrushchev based themselves on the idea that our huge defense expenditures would bring about an American financial collapse. But the Soviet Union has gone broke first. They never thought of that!

Women and the menu

I HAVE yet to understand what goes on in a woman's mind when she goes into a good restaurant. She will insist on eating the most unappetizing food possible. Any proprietor ingenius enough to put tripe on the menu endears himself forever. Ask a woman about it and she will say, "When we go out to a restaurant we want to eat food we don't eat at home." Do they think any sane, healthy, normal, patriotic American citizen would ever eat tête-de-veau at home? Those meals were all invented because France was once a poor country and they ate everything on the cow. You cannot convince her that any healthy, normal, patriotic Frenchman, given his choice, disdains tête-de-veau and prefers tournedos.

There are some women addicted to the goofy selection like other women are addicted to tranquilizers. Take a woman to a steak house and invariably she will choose the shish-kabob. The men eat the porterhouse or the strip sirloin or the T-bone, but the women go for the rice pilaf. Apple pie and cheese will never do for dessert. Never. It's got to be a baked pear with raisins.

Ordering a shrimp cocktail with a steak is a personal affront to most wives, especially on their anniversaries. They give you that look they reserve for gas station attendants who tell them they've been driving the car with no water in the radiator.

A woman in a restaurant is a complex mechanism. No explanation like, "I prefer steak," or "Goulash is my dish," suffices. If you love her, you have to love sweetbreads and crab bisque.

It is my belief that if the rest of the world ate off the bottom of the menu, they would long ago have been overwhelmed by the Russians. It's the fellows who eat roast beef instead of beef heart and steak instead of oxtails who dream up such ideas as the Declaration of Independence and the Common Market.

The short, cool summers

In 1934, a Beckwith Evans would not even have been arrested for killing a Negro; in 1944, he would have been arrested but not tried; in 1954, he would have been arrested, tried, and acquitted; in 1964, we at least had two hung juries. This is gradualism!

Circumventing the censors

JACK NELSON and Gene Roberts, Jr., two outstanding newspapermen, have collaborated on a book which they call *The Censors and the Schools*.

"In music," according to the official DAR report published in this book, "too many 'work tunes' and 'folk songs' were found."

The school authorities of Charlotte, North Carolina, have a

system. As soon as any self-styled patriot makes a complaint about a "subversive" textbook in the schools, the teachers mail off a questionnaire which includes such questions as: Have you read the book? To what passages does your complaint refer? In what way are the passages offensive? What do you know of the author? Which of his other books have you read?

It is a pretty effective system for preserving peace. One thing book-burners don't like to do is read books and answer questions.

On getting old

No ONE wants to get old, but we do desire to become older. We enjoy the advantages without the limited disadvantages, and that is important as we journey into the sixth decade.

To enjoy life with congenial work and interesting associates, to outwit pains and aches and a depressed state of mind, is the prescription best suited for us.

Many things have lost their charm, and other things must be given up. To be inactive is to find deterioration. To overeat is to drive the body and we must remember we acquired this model a generation before the Essex car went out of business. We need to learn to like new things, a baked potato with a dash of Worcestershire sauce is a new epicurean delight. It is full of vitamins and Irish bounce, just what the doctor ordered. The glass of buttermilk, also Irish fare, and you are all set again.

Meeting interesting people and yet having time for a walk means taking them on the walk, or meeting them at the party by prearrangement instead of in a smoking shop or office.

All the old people learned delightful ways to enjoy life—
Herbert Hoover, Carl Sandburg, Robert Frost, Harry Truman,
Bernard Baruch, Winston Churchill.

We waited untold eons of time to arrive here. Why not live
it up?

The futility of war

MOST philosophers have been pacifists since, dealing
with ideas as they do, they have been able to visualize a world
without war. Philosophers are not only able to add up ideas
but to subtract them, too.

For one hundred and fifty years, Germany dreamt and
talked of *"lebensraum"*—breathing room for her growing population. Germany looked toward the Ukraine, the "bread
basket" of Europe, and argued that an industrial power needs
wheat. Many non-Germans felt sorry for Germany. And on
three occasions—1870, 1914, and 1939—Germany started
tearing the world apart for *lebensraum*. Today Germany is no
closer to *lebensraum* than ever. She is no place near the
Ukraine. Yet Germany is better off than anyone ever thought
possible. Germans eat better and have more things than they
had under Bismarck, the Kaiser, and Hitler.

Japan also felt sorry for herself. She was an island, isolated.
She had entered Western civilization at a disadvantage which
she hoped to redress by grabbing off Korea. After Korea, Japan
said plaintively she could not exist without an Asian co-prosperity sphere. Vainly she started aggressive war. Not only does
Japan not have an Asian co-prosperity sphere, not only does
she not have Korea, she doesn't even control Okinawa, one of
her home islands. But Japan never had it so good.

And England had her Empiah! The Empiah upon which, as Malcolm Muggeridge put it, the sun never rose. Yet the time came when England had to surrender India and instead of Suez, Englishmen have the "Never, Never" plan of installment buying (so called because no purchase is ever really paid off). It made no difference whether or not England owned Suez. The only income Egypt really gets from the Suez Canal is from the British ships which steam through. Without Britain, three hundred rich Egyptian families would join eight million other Egyptian families living in abject poverty.

For the Koreans to own a transistor radio they send Japan the raw materials, those very raw materials Japan had to dig herself when she owned Korea. It is a lot easier and more profitable to sit home and make transistor radios than to occupy a strange land and scout up iron ore.

France thought the world would end were she to lose Algeria and were the Foreign Legion to abandon Sidi-bel-Abbès. Young Frenchmen for generations wasted their seed somewhere in Indo-China or Africa, or Syria, or Madagascar. Young French girls, deprived of the chance to get a husband, took to frequenting Montmartre and walking the other streets of Paris.

But in the next half century, France will grow up and her growth won't all be nourished by Charles de Gaulle. Her growth will be nourished because Frenchmen between the ages of eighteen and thirty-five will be home instead of idling away their lives in Indo-China, Madagascar, Syria, and Algeria.

Think of the manhood slaughtered for such empty ideas as *lebensraum*, Empiah, Algerie Française. And these warring nations are discovering what Americans, whether by accidental design or providential protection, learned years ago. Keep the boys at home. They will make more money, more children, and more history that way. It is America's anti-colonial tradition

that made her great. Even when she has to send men to the
Philippines, Europe, Africa, and Asia, she limits service to
eighteen months. Pentagon, Shmentagon, there's lots of wisdom around this country, naïve as Europeans may think we
are.

Machismo

"MACHISMO" is one of the great philosophic concepts
to come to us from Puerto Rico. It is not, as yet, the rage
among intellectuals and it may never be popular—but all of us
know the impact of an idea has nothing to do with its validity.

Newton didn't discover gravity when the apple fell upon his
head; all he discovered was a way to name the phenomenon
which made the apple fall. Machismo is a phenomenon much
like gravity. It compels and guides and determines us, but
only the Puerto Ricans have been hit on the head with it.

I came across this phenomenon in a discussion I had recently with several officials of the New York City Youth
Board. They remarked on the curious fact that in paternity
cases a majority of the Negroes, Jews, Italians, Armenians,
Hungarians, Poles, Greeks, Anglo-Saxons, including Irishmen,
Scotsmen, Germans, and English, not only deny responsibility but go so far as to say they never saw the woman before. But not the Puerto Rican. He not only admits he knows
the girl about whom he may or may not care, but is volubly
insistent it darn well is his child, and somebody better not
say differently. Raising any doubts about his being the father
of a child would be raising doubts about his machismo.

Roughly translated and roughly explained, machismo is the
philosophy of "I am a MAN, darn it, and don't forget it,

either." And he'll waste no opportunity to confirm it. It pervades all of Puerto Rican life. It makes a woman proud to know this. That is why there are so many happy marriages in Puerto Rico.

The situation is interesting in Italy, too. Indro Montanelli, Italian writer, says the Italian cinema, novel, play, and public square are filled with erotic behavior and display for the simple reason that Italian men and women have never learned how to speak to one another. He recites how Italians have never had the institution of the salon where cultivated men and women exchanged sophisticated attitudes nor did they have a frontier where the woman helped in the spring plowing. To this day, he says, the only "communication" between Italian men and women is in the bed.

Look how lucky we American men are: we get to share supermarket shopping with the little woman. We get to pluck cake mixes and baby foods from the pretty shelves. We get to discuss budgets, spouse to spouse, an ever-continuing mathematic experience.

We share so many more things: all of us men and women can go to P.T.A. meetings and then we have a common parliamentry procedure which is nothing if not discussable. Men and women in America generate a hysterical tension and anxiety about the children, or the school system, or the healthy environment, and this welds us together.

It all goes to show how much wiser we have been than the Italians. No Italian madonna makes out the income tax return for the family, nor for that matter does any Italian madonna keep the checking account in order.

Here in the Land of the Free we let our teen-agers get together early in life and they talk about "going steady," and about the newest recording and clothes, all of which prepares them for a life of happy spiritual communion.

It is only curious that our divorce rate is so much higher than Italy's and our asylums so much more overcrowded.

Passion in perspective

ONE of our national magazines which shall be nameless (I have called that magazine nameless so many times I have come to think that must be its name) ran a lengthy article called "Sex in the United States."

I have no wish to cavil with some of the conclusions but I did note certain discrepancies.

Any discussion of sex is perforce a discussion of the young. The young, said the nameless magazine, "seem earnestly trying to construct their own code, and are even discovering for themselves some of the older verities."

I really doubt the young move in any sort of social concert. One look at the songs the young prefer indicate their chief interest is how lonely they are. It is somewhat mistaken to think they communicate rapidly and articulately with each other.

When the Army football team, which is representative certainly of the young, was on the Navy two-yard line, did they send Joe Waldrop off tackle as everybody knew they ought to? Indeed they did not. They huddled to find out what they ought to do, with the result they did nothing. The clock ran out and Navy won.

I cannot bring myself to believe the young have a movement afoot to place sex in a proper perspective. It is true that the young answer questionnaires about their sexual activities or the lack of it but they only prove that polltakers are bad judges of who is lying.

Articles on the sex life of Americans seem pointless to me because the national experience, at least in statistics, is so remote from one's own. Indeed, even though moralistic in tone, these résumés seem to have no influence.

The week this article appeared, a group of doctors in a conference out in California said that wives ought to let husbands roam if they want the family to survive.

I doubt these doctors would have sent Waldrop off tackle either.

Just what kind of a relationship is a fellow going to establish with his sweetie if he tells her, "My wife understands me. That's why I'm on the town tonight"? What self-respecting housebreaker would respond to this? Where's the challenge? Where's the adventure?

Sometimes I wonder if the folks are out cavorting at all. I think the large majority are home reading the Kinsey Reports and articles about their mischief in Nameless Magazine. Frankly, with the time consumed by the P.T.A. meetings and the family budget I don't see where they get the time.

The doors we open

THERE are doors we open every day and find ourselves staring at a brick wall. We wonder, "Indeed! Now why did I open that door?" but the thought never deters us from opening another.

I think of the admission we all make. "Everyone has his own faults and I have mine." On close inspection, however, each of us says, "I really can't list my faults. I am not violently short-tempered nor particularly selfish, nor am I malicious or a gossip." I suspect the reason we confess to nameless faults is because we know the fellow to whom we confess is laden with faults.

Another of these brick walls is the desperate phone call. Your lawyer, wife, best friend, on the other end says urgently, "I've got to see you. Something terrible has happened."

"What? What has happened?"

I can't discuss it on the phone."

There are literally hundreds of thousands of little old ladies living off the dividends paid by A. T. & T., but the crucial moment in life cannot be discussed over the telephone. These little old ladies will tell you that is what the telephone is there for.

This has transpired over my phone so often I am adept at gauging how serious the trouble is. If the fellow says, "I can't discuss it on the phone," it's about money and if he says, "I can't tell you over the phone," it's about women. Invariably the worst offender is the fellow whose monthly phone bill is in excess of four figures. He can do everything on the telephone except help himself.

The last of these brick walls I propose to discuss is the phrase "Come see us." I heard it when I first came south, and in those naïve, salad days I presumed when people said, "Come see us," they meant come to their house and see them. That is not what it means at all in Dixie. It means "So long," or, "Nice to have seen you this morning," or, "Bye bye," because I have never heard it uttered with a specific date.

Life is not casual about those who end every conversation, "Come see us soon." Indeed not. Conversation is casual.

I have decided when someone says, "We all have our faults," to reply, "Not me. Amen." And to the urgent phone caller whose dire message cannot be entrusted to impersonal wires, to say, "Look, whatever is so important can wait. Put it in the mail." And to the third, "Come see us," the succinct rejoinder,

"I am terribly busy for the next few months, but will New Year's Eve do?"

Joy and sorrow

WEEPING for joy and weeping for sorrow explain only the motives in weeping. One is as much agony as another.

The paradoxical quality of human nature is that great joy often overwhelms and subdues and breaks down a man with more effect than great sorrow. Your children making their first Communion; your boy speaking at his *bar mitzvah;* your daughter walking toward the altar or the wedding canopy—often that which should be the happiest moment in a lifetime produces the one break in human reserve.

I remember a big theatrical affair in honor of William Fox and Marcus Loew, two of the pioneers in the motion picture industry. Both had been immigrants and sweatshop workers in their early years. The great movie stars whom they had helped create were all there, blowing kisses to the guests of honor. Finally the big moment. From opposite wings came Fox and Loew to meet in the center of the stage for a few words of fellowship and appreciation. But as they looked at each other and shook hands they began to weep, and they wept bitterly. They never regained control, and the audience rose as a man and wept along with them.

When Colgate W. Darden was inaugurated governor, I remember watching Darden's old father weeping. In his time this elderly Virginia aristocrat must have survived with dignity many heartaches and moments of deep sorrow and grief. The pride of watching his son accept the oath of office stripped him of his reserve, and probably for the first time in many, many years.

The reason for this, I think, is that we suppose all the bad breaks are in the cards, that's how the game is played. We steel ourselves to play as well as we can against losing propositions. The unexpected subdues us. The unexpected glory or accomplishment hits us with the same force as the things we don't want to happen, but where we expect the death of a loved one, or bankruptcy, or failure, we are not always morally prepared for sudden happiness.

Moral effect of the gutter

MY PARENTS never discussed sex with children. Neither, for that matter, did any other parent on the Lower East Side and, as far as I can determine, throughout the country generally. The kids picked up the knowledge they had to have from "the gutter" and from the crude scrawls on backyard fences.

The psychiatrists, social workers, psychologists and family counselors deplored this method. Nowadays, parents discuss these matters with children. As a result, illegitimate births have risen almost thirty percent since the turn of the century and the statistics for juvenile delinquency are running away from the computers.

The retired

THEY sit on the benches and discuss their ailments: "I haven't had a letter from daughter since Mother's Day." "I couldn't hear the sermon today, but it's not my hearing aid, it's the electrical connection in the church."

This is what we do with the aged: we shove them into an incubator where they wait vegetable-like for the small joys of isolated life, fretting about all the annoyances of the day. I've watched them with interest and dismay in special enclaves for "the retired" in Southern California, Florida, and suburbs of Chicago, New York, Asheville, and Tucson.

They are terribly worried about children and dogs. Both mean noise. They investigate carefully before they rent or buy to make sure there are no children or no dogs on the block. The happily giggling child is an object of hostility as though they object to his youth and would deprive him of it.

Our businessmen urge the aged to give up all ties and roots and buy into these inexpensive yet depressing developments. For that reason, the old are cranky and we blame them. The New England grandma may be cranky, but she was probably sour as a girl, too. Where the old live surrounded by the middle-aged and the young, they live happier and longer.

But in these special developments for "the retired" they ask, "Isn't it time for lunch?" The question is first put at 10:15 and is continued until 11:50. And the old men will beat with their canes the hood of a car which has parked two inches over the white dividing lines.

Waiting on a man

Nothing takes the place in a woman's life of waiting on a man. It gives her high purpose. She is never unemployed, as a normal male usually loses buttons, breaks shoelaces, misplaces cuff links, forgets to buy razor blades, cannot find his pipe, and left his pen right here and it's gone and where are the keys to the car?

The mourning of a widow is because she is no longer needed. The dismal order of quietude! That is why the women try to keep the boys going along toward the one hundred and twentieth birthday.

Uncle Hymie and best-sellers

WRITING successful books establishes a relationship among friends and relatives that is *sui generis*.

Take my Uncle Hymie, now in his seventy-fifth year. For over forty years, or as long as he has been reading English, Uncle Hymie read only the house organ of the International Ladies Garment Workers Union. He was an official of that organization before his retirement eight years ago. He kept up with the news of the world in the Yiddish press, Uncle Hymie being among the last of that vanishing breed who were stalwarts of the Yiddish press, theatre, and literature.

But ever since I wrote *Only in America*, Uncle Hymie has read with consuming interest the book sections of the entire metropolitan press and the *Saturday Review*.

"How come," he asks me, "Dutton has run four ads on four successive Sundays and your publisher has run only one?" Uncle Hymie is now thoroughly conversant with the publishing trade jargon and with every publisher's spring and fall list. He regards each publisher as a personal threat to me, his nephew, and to him, my uncle. "I don't know why they gave Vance Packard such a good review," he will tell me, or "Read one Herman Wouk, you've read them all." His voice on these occasions sounds shaky, as though Vance Packard and Herman Wouk were pointing separate pistols at our joint heads.

And he watches those best-seller lists like a hawk. If a book of mine has a short stay on that list, Uncle Hymie acts as though I had offered him a mortal affront, as though I, personally, were the cause for his mortification! When I meet him, he is diplomatic on the subject, but the concern is there.

Nor is he above offering postmortem advice. "I don't think you should have included that story about Southern politics," he says. "It hurt sales. It didn't do us any good."

Over and above these admonitions is Uncle Hymie's constant expectation and trepidation. He is worried about other publishers, other writers, all reviewers, and always the next book. "Tell me," says Uncle Hymie. "I see where Random House and Knopf have some fine non-fiction coming out. How do you think we'll do this year?"

For anonymous callers

THE RIGHT makes the anonymous telephone calls.

You never heard a member of the Far Right (or just plain Right) complain of anonymous phone calls, because it is they who make the calls.

The moment your name appears in the press with an expression against capital punishment, or *for* the United Nations, integration, medicare, and fluoridation, the *rightists* take to the telephone, in droves; many just call every few minutes and hang up. They think they are breaking your spirit. But others pour out a torrent of obscene abuse.

In recent years I have used a pretty good system, which I

recommend to others similarly annoyed. For the fellows who pour out the obscenities I say: "Wait a minute, you have the wrong party, this is [and here I always use the name of the most recent winner of the Man-of-the-Year Award, widely publicized by the afternoon paper and the Chamber of Commerce]." This usually makes the fellow hesitate; he bangs up the phone; he thinks he dialed the wrong number. The phone rings a second later; the jerk dialed more carefully this time. But I know who it is and I say loudly, "So-and-so [current Man of the Year] speaking!" The fellow bangs up the phone in disgust, confused—I hope.

Chicken soup vs. peanut butter

TWO STORIES, which could have had tragic endings, ended happily recently. One little boy who was lost in New York's Central Park was found tired and hungry, but unharmed. Two little girls accidentally locked themselves in a bathroom in an apartment building in Virginia. They, too, were weary and hungry when finally found.

The thing that struck me about the reports of these instances was the first meals of these youngsters. No sooner had they reached home than their mothers sat them down and gave them a meal: the girls had peanut butter sandwiches and milk; the boy had peanut butter sandwiches and strawberry soda pop.

What's with this peanut butter? In my day it was chicken soup. But this was far from being an "immigrant" habit. The fifth-generation Southerners tell me that for them, too, the cure-all was chicken broth.

The kids, I understand, love peanut butter. When Junior doesn't eat his meat and potatoes, I find young mothers shrugging their shoulders and saying, "All right, I'll fix you a peanut butter sandwich."

The fond memory of chicken soup in all these situations is not mere sentimentality. It was good for everything from hunger to a Charley horse.

But today it is peanut butter, and let us not stand in the way of progress. I even noticed on television the other night that a commercial was pushing peanut butter not for children, but for parents. Grown-ups, they were saying, love peanut butter, too.

There are two kinds of peanut butter, I find. There is a smooth or creamy style and there is a crunchy brand with peanuts mixed in.

What the commercials don't say is that peanut butter can be the devil on some of us with loose upper plates. If we ever get lost in the park, I am afraid it will have to be "a nice bowl of hot chicken soup."

True short stories

THERE has been an upturn for the better in the real-estate business in Charlotte, and one of the more enterprising agents betook himself out to the country scouting for acreage.

He came across a beautiful old house with lovely rolling fields surrounding it and talked to the owner. The old lady was quite friendly and she told him her family had lived there ever since her grandfather settled on the land in 1850.

Looking at the well-kept house and the flourishing fields, the agent cocked his head and said, "Yessiree, lady, you sure have got it made."

To which the elderly woman replied: "At eighty-three I've got it made? What kind of a stupid ass are you anyway? At eighty-three you think I've got it made?" And with that she slammed the door in his face.

*   *   *

Marjorie didn't like the richly conservative and comfortable furnishings in the large, pleasant home of her parents, Jack and Betty Cohen. After a long debate, eighteen-year-old Marjorie had her way and their home had a new look, everything was Danish modern, and Betty felt like a stranger in her own home and her husband Jack missed the big, slightly soiled easy chair.

Now Marjorie is married to a very nice boy, Sam Goldman, and while Sam is serving his internship at a local hospital they are living in a one-room apartment over a garage which is furnished with her parents' old furniture, including her father's favorite easy chair.

*   *   *

Milton and Elaine had adjoining desks at Amalgamated Petroleum. They became engaged, as people at adjoining desks often do. They stayed engaged for eleven years, for Milton had many reasons for postponing the marriage—his father was ill; his brother was in college; he didn't make enough. Then his father died, his brother Sid was graduated and married, and he got a raise and a cost-of-living bonus.

Still no marriage.

On one of his vacations, he eloped. A mean office worker put the notice on Elaine's desk. She covered her typewriter and left immediately. The office worried. Elaine was in a desperate mood. Would she harm herself?

Elaine came back—but what an Elaine! New dress, new hairdo, nails exquisite, lips and cheeks glowing—in short, she was stunning.

Harry, the boss's son, thought she was a wow. When Milton came back from his honeymoon he found Elaine had also eloped. Now, in fact, he was working for her husband.

Elaine comes to every office party, gracious and kind despite her mink and diamonds and always with a nod for Milton, who sits at the same desk getting the same cost-of-living bonus.

Harry is proud of his wife and makes speeches about how he loves her and his handsome sons and how wise he was to have plucked the pearl of Amalgamated Petroleum instead of some empty-headed society girl. Everyone thinks this is good reasoning. Everyone except Milton, but no one asks Milton what he thinks.

* * *

I remember a poet living in the old Markwell Hotel in New York, where I was a clerk, who not only starved but dodged his bills that he might write tightly constructed sonnets. One short story in the *Saturday Evening Post*, however, landed him a contract as a Hollywood writer. He paid up and as he was leaving I commiserated with him, saying, "I wish you luck, but it's too bad about your poetry."

"What poetry?" said this émigré. "Never mind the poetry. I can't wait to get my hands on that money and them long-legged starlets."

There was a writer for you.

Etiquette for teen-agers

Boys and girls go to school together because, presumably, as adults they will have to live together. But I am not sure this logic isn't specious. After all, as adults, they will not be going to school: living with one another is enough of a strain.

On the Lower East Side of New York City, P.S. 91 was for girls and P.S. 20 was for boys. The boys went to DeWitt Clinton High School and the girls went to Wadleigh High.

Coeducation, I believe, is one of the most inopportune innovations in the history of learning, particularly at the high school level. It has done nothing but turn the high school into a social club. The girls are concerned with their dresses and their hairdos, and the boys with getting cars and athletic letters so the girls with their pretty dresses and their well-teased hairdos will go steady with them.

Going to school is the biggest thing that can happen to anybody. It ought not to be alloyed with the problems of social adaptation which in turn lead to worse problems like those of teen-age marriage.

The late Bernard Berenson, the world-famous art critic, says in his memoirs that while in Harvard he preferred the conversation of William James and other professors to that of his fellow students. The professors not only knew more but were more accessible than the students. Nothing, he wrote, is so ridiculously exclusive and cliquey as the Anglo-Saxon schoolboy. You can imagine how sorry it is when we let schoolboys and schoolgirls ape adult manners, which are already gauche, without giving them a chance to grow into a proper appreciation of the adult world.

In a recent issue of *Datebook*, "a magazine for aware teen-agers," a mother writes:

> I want my daughter to go steady. . . . You'd think it was something far worse than juvenile delinquency or narcotics addiction the way some people harangue against going steady. . . . I say baloney. . . . I say leave them alone. . . . I say if going steady has become a problem it is because adults took it too seriously in the first place.

She continues:

> If adults devoted themselves a little more to the real problems of their day—higher pay for teachers, nuclear disarmament—perhaps they wouldn't be imposing yesterday's adult values on today's healthy children.

I'm not quite sure what that last sentence means, if anything, but we'll let it go. Going steady is not only here to stay, but it has its champions.

Going steady is the result of the wonders of our middle-class living. The kids are no dumbbells. They want it now. Margaret Mead reports that some teen-agers have found a way to get it fast if parental largesse is slow. The girl gets pregnant and that settles that.

Romantic love, or that love which summons us one and all to the marriage altar, is an invention of the Middle Ages; it specifically descends from the age of chivalry. It is that complex of emotions and biological urges which made of a woman a "precious object."

I fail to see that "going steady" is any refinement upon the original. It seems to me, in fact, a debasement. After all, the knights had to ride horses and write sonnets and gallop round the castles where the lady fair lived, while all a boy has to do today is borrow Pop's car and he and his steady tool down the thruway.

The ecstasy of partnership and the joy of love at an age when you can afford it momentarily hold no wonders for the kids.

By the time she is twenty-one the only new thrill left for the girl would be to go down to the waterfront and get tattooed.

For that long part of a lifetime before this happens—say five years—there is some guidance available.

The magazine *Seventeen* has published a new book on etiquette for the teen-agers. It tells them how to conduct themselves right up to "the climax"—a good way to plan for a perfect marriage.

Along with this valuable information comes a perfect recipe for the teen-ager "at-home" party. The menu includes ham, asparagus rolls, cream cheese and date-nut bars. During the party, it is all right for Miss Teen-age to break up boys huddling together. She can do this most easily by interrupting them to speak to young Mr. Boyfriend.

But what to do about parents? The teen-age etiquette answers: "After everyone has arrived, the parents ought to disappear to another part of the house." What I think the manners experts mean is that it would be very convenient if the parents simply disappeared after preparing the asparagus rolls.

In perusing the teen-age etiquette, please note the "sixteen-point plan for making good on the college or prep school weekend." No parent dare interfere with this any more than a parent would dare say no to the asparagus rolls. Years ago, teenagers argued with parents, which was in itself a natural thing, but no teen-ager ever gossiped about his parents or anyone else's. They didn't tell friends that their mother was "hysterical" and they never said of their father he was a "square."

The one thing this book doesn't tell teen-agers is "How to get rid of your parents in twelve easy stages."

Eisenhower and the moon

IN THE course of remarks at the Pinehurst Country Club, in North Carolina, President Eisenhower condemned the nation's moon-race as a "fifty-billion-dollar gamble."

We have very little information to go along with the former President's opinion or to argue against it.

I think the only pertinent comment would be a sigh of relief that Franklin Roosevelt was in the White House when Albert Einstein wrote his letter about heavy water and nuclear fission.

Can you imagine the Republicans gambling four billion dollars on a letter from an egghead who never met a payroll?

A secret therapy

IT STRIKES me that with the immense discoveries in plastic materials and manufacturing techniques, not to mention the new paper processes and plastics, we could get rid of washing the dishes if we chose. We could make all the dishes out of plastic or paper with the appropriate dinnerware patterns, and when we had finished eating simply roll them all up in the plastic tablecloth and out—no more dishpan hands. No more hurrying with the soap and suds and missing vital segments of the evening's TV programs.

This is not what has happened. Instead of there being fewer

dishes these days, there are more. There are even salad bowls you don't wash but have to wipe.

Obviously the world does not wish to get rid of the dish-washing chore. It may well be that some of the ladies want to assert their dominance by having some of the husbands dry.

I suspect, however, that washing the dishes is one of the less appreciated therapies. Even putting the dishes in the dish-washer is a therapy. It is virtually part of the digestive process itself. We say grace before dinner and wash the dishes after. Come to think of it, washing the dishes may be one of those stabilizing influences the American family has during these trying times of dope addiction, delinquency, and high school dropouts.

One of the times I tried eating without washing up after-ward still haunts me. I went off with some friends to the Great Smoky Mountains of North Carolina for a three-day rest. Since it did nothing but rain, we never went outdoors but spent a profitable weekend playing pinochle and eating man-sized steaks. Sunday night we drew straws to see who would wash the dishes. This was no simple chore. It meant schlep-ping the water from the well, building a fire to heat it and then immersing the dishes.

Another fellow and I got the short straws. So what we did, in order to get back to the pinochle game, was bury all the dishes and the silverware.

Woman's saga

IN HER twenties a woman needs health.

In her thirties a woman needs personality.

In her forties she needs money.

Troubled sons and daughters

In CHARLOTTE the other night two boy vandals were arrested for driving back and forth over some lawns. The ground was badly torn and, of course, the azaleas and the crocuses and the shrubs were ruined.

The police discovered that these boys had been riding around with two girls and had later parked on a lonely road.

For the last decade these kids had been exposed to the image of the virile male and sexy female in the movies and in the advertisements, and the stars who have convinced the kids that sex is passionate and facile.

Then they get in the back seat of the automobile and they discover that sex is not facile nor passionate. Probably not even satisfactory. Probably there were only fumbling attempts at sex rather than sex itself. They do not realize that this is quite normal and so they become distressed. The boy thinks there may be something wrong with him; the girl asks, "Is that all there is to it?"

The kids are convinced they are inadequate rather than that the image is a lie. For sex is a basic human relationship, and more than ardor and enthusiasm, it needs maturity. But none of us is so beautiful as the ladies in our ads or so glamorous as the women in the television bubble bath, none of us is so sophisticated as the typist in the liquor ads or so powerful as the hero of a Western movie. Ergo, the kids are impotent—if not physically, spiritually.

The car therefore becomes not only a symbol but a source of power, and shouting "Zoom" and ravaging a neighbor's lawn eases the frustration.

Mothers and daughters

FAILURE is the only result for the mothers and daughters who have become pals in this generation. In my generation, even when the daughter was preparing her trousseau, Mother never held any intimate discussions with her. An aunt did this, or perhaps a married sister. There was an aloofness between mother and daughter and I'm not so sure it wasn't the better system. I have known mothers and daughters who are pals. The girls grow up in an atmosphere of revelation. The idea is to tell your parents *everything* and if you tell them *everything* "they will understand." This is the first big mistake. The mother loses the identity of a parent and becomes a confidante and often an accomplice. It's the generation of pals —and the parents have lost the authority and the respect our parents before us had.

This has little to do with our morality or the morality of parents generations ago. Discuss wild oats with your mother and father? Heaven forbid. It is part of the idea of "freedom" but it is not really freedom. In one home I know the daughter comes home from college and gossips with her mother, hour after hour, about which of her classmates is going with a boy or living with a boy and which of her classmates is on pills. This is a big deal today, who's on pills. The palsy-walsy deal, I'm afraid, has not paid off.

The emancipated woman

IN THE beginning she found herself able to travel only at her children's speed, and was additionally handicapped by

birth at any time of the year. She learned therefore to attach
herself to an adult male who in turn found safety in the young
male hunters she produced and comfort in the firewood and
garments her daughters provided. In the next few thousand
years she learned how to reduce the male's speed to her own
leisurely pace, and this became her passport through life. No
matter the extent of her accomplishments, she has no "visa"
without a male. The Hebrews have a word which is never uttered except in an inaudible whisper, "*agunah*" (the forsaken),
and it still strikes terror in the heart of every Jewish woman
throughout the world. All the essays on the life, the hope, and
the destiny of the "American woman," or of any woman anywhere, may be reduced to a single phrase—"Please don't ever
leave me."

When Sigmund Freud left Clark University in New York
to go home to Vienna, he remarked America's great experiment was the liberation of its women. He didn't think it
would work, though.

I wonder if he was not right.

England produced an Elizabeth I and a Victoria. It is true
both were drafted into greatness, but great ages bear their
names. Certainly Florence Nightingale is one of history's great
women. She not only entered nursing in the days when its
only practitioners were prostitutes, but she reformed and bent
to her will that most hidebound of all modern institutions,
the British Army. Woman suffrage was still a dream when
she died.

Russia had Catherine the Great, who, libertine and reac-
tionary though she was, still set up the Russian bureaucracy, a
system so efficient it has persevered right through Khrushchev's
time.

Jeanne d'Arc unified France and became its patron saint.

Madame Curie was instrumental in the understanding of radium and radioactivity. Egypt had Cleopatra.

Only Greece, Rome, and America come to mind as civilizations which did not produce historical women of destiny. The nearest we Americans have come to a great woman, I suppose, is Eleanor Roosevelt. Her greatness lay in her humanity and advocacy of reforms, and her humanity and advocacy were significant because she was the wife of Franklin D. Roosevelt.

We could say Abraham Lincoln's beloved stepmother, Sarah Bush, was great in that she had a hand in shaping greatness, but I suspect what we really mean about Mrs. Roosevelt and Sarah Bush is that they were heroic, which is different from greatness.

"Think of the suffragettes!" some of my readers will urge. What I think is that Ellen Glasgow and Emily Brontë accomplished more without the vote than most women accomplish with it.

A culture produces great women when the women are sure they are loved.

Women entertain the erroneous idea that before the twentieth century, they were all vassals. But women were always deferred to. For nothing has ever prevailed against the institution of marriage, not even easy divorce laws. Women always ran the house or the castle or the hut. Life itself may have been rude but it treated women less rudely than it treated everyone else.

Cleopatra never looked through a microscope nor did Queen Victoria spend her summer vacations painting sets at the local theater. Yet they were great women, great because not only were they loved, but the mass of women in their societies were loved.

I never remember my mother sitting back on her chair. She always sat on its edge. I don't believe she ever ate a whole meal. But when I was older and asked her why, she replied, "I sit on the edge of my chair six nights a week so that on the Sabbath I am the Queen." Her experience was duplicated hundreds of thousands of times.

There was one basic system our mothers followed. The father would ask her advice, something about the family, the prospective son-in-law, or even about a change of jobs or a new business venture, and the mother always said, "I have only a woman's brain which is not much, but I would suggest so-and-so." And so-and-so was always adopted—that is, when the father was a man of wisdom. She made certain that the father saved face as the boss, but she ran the works.

One of the big worries among the immigrant Orthodox women on the Lower East Side was that their presence would fill the thoughts of their men and distract them from their work and their study of the Talmud. With minor modifications, I believe this has been the case in many past societies. It is the happiest worry a woman can have. But this worry is dissipated. No woman is retiring these days but more and more are anonymous.

Once upon a time, women did not grin at us from every page in a newspaper or parade in their lingerie through the editorial pages and on to the obituaries. They did not cavort in bathing suits on billboards nor did they deodorize themselves on television every hour on the half hour.

Though we have liberated women, allowed them to pursue their own aspirations, given them the ballot and elevated them to political office, made many of them millionairesses by virtue of their faces or their legs, we do not have great women because we cannot separate the girl from her natural functions. And apparently very few girls want to be separated. I mean this in no jest.

Soon—the spring

YOU in the North no doubt have your complaints, but you can't imagine what a blizzard or heavy snowfall or sleet storm is like in the South. We don't have enough storms to justify the capital outlay for snowplows and cleaners. When storms come we are tied up forever. One time, I remember, we had to call the Fire Department to get the girls from the office home (I offered all and any a night's lodging, but they took their chances on the fire truck).

Spring means poetry and Sandy Koufax. It does an old man's heart good to read about all those young ballplayers out in Arizona and down in Florida pulling their muscles and suffering sprains and breaks and sweating off what is euphemistically called "winter poundage." How so many injury-prone fellows could get into the sport beats me, but they do.

It has always amazed me that so few poets are baseball fans. The game itself is a marvel of symmetry and grace. It abounds in courage and determination. I was never so encouraged as when old man Harvey Haddix pitched twelve scoreless innings against the Milwaukee Braves several years ago.

Poets are certainly fans of the spring. But baseball is represented by "Casey at the Bat," an epic which only Tallulah Bankhead can possibly make acceptable.

We think we are immortal

WE THINK we are immortal and that is why automotive, refrigerative, missile, and cosmetic technology has so outstripped medical and pharmaceutical research.

At the peak of our mental and imaginative powers we can apply ourselves to new processes of steel construction, we can easily imagine different ways of marketing glamor, and we can compute our passage to the moon. At this age most of us think we will live forever, if we think about life at all. Why should we die, we who are so strong, who fill life with energy, work, and thinking?

When we grow old and realize our powers have diminished, then it is too late. Intimations of death are upon us. Why did we not use our faculties to concentrate on how to regenerate tissue, strengthen the heart, abolish the degenerative diseases? Alas, we did not. Our sons tell their friends, "The care Dad gets in the Allendale Home is wonderful. He is content. He plays checkers daily with his cronies. Truly, his life is all an old man could ask . . . much better than my wife and I could do for him at home, blah, blah, blah."

Medical science has today conquered the diseases that ravaged mankind. We have brought malaria and rickets under control, rid the world for the most part of the bubonic plague, no one dies any more of diptheria or pneumonia. But the degenerative diseases are yet to be conquered. Science has yet to master the chemical imbalances of the body that result in cancer, hardening of the arteries, heart stoppages. A crash program would solve all of these. But the billions for crash programs are dedicated to cars that go faster, iceboxes that make an endless supply of cubes, makeup that is ever more alluring, and missiles that will carry whole armies.

We need these things, because we think we are immortal.

Churchill

ONE OF the compensations of this terrible time in which we live is that we have been Winston Churchill's contemporaries. We have looked upon the face of greatness in our time.

Harold MacMillan, former Prime Minister, told his colleagues in the House of Commons that the old men among them knew they had never seen the like of Churchill and that the young men just starting would never see the like again.

Call me a wild man. Call me Mr. Exaggeration. Were it not for Winston Churchill I do not believe we would have a governor of North Carolina today, or a governor of any of the other forty-nine states. Were it not for Winston Churchill millions of us now living would be dead. Were it not for Winston Churchill the United States of America would be an entirely different country today, ruled by Nazi *Gauleiters* on orders from Berlin and Berchtesgarden. I believe all of this with all my heart.

PART 2

Sojourner Truth and Gene Young

Sojourner Truth and Gene Young

SOJOURNER TRUTH was a Negro slave who had been sold several times but who obtained her freedom with the passage of New York's Emancipation Act in 1829. She spent the rest of her life campaigning against the inhuman terrors of slavery, making speeches all over the country.

On one occasion she spoke in an Indiana city controlled by the pro-slavery Copperheads, political forebears of the Mississippi-Alabama segregationists. The leading Copperhead was a physician who spread the rumor that Sojourner Truth was a man in woman's disguise. On the evening she spoke, the pro-slavery faction was in the hall en masse, prepared to heckle her. Sojourner Truth had heard the rumor and before she began, the gaunt middle-aged black woman removed her blouse and said, "These breasts have nursed black children some, but they nursed more white children." The audience sat spellbound as the Confederate sympathizers slowly filed out.

One hundred years later, the Negro boy Gene Young couldn't wait for President Johnson to sign the Civil Rights Act of 1964. He ran down to the barbershop of the grand old Muehlebach Hotel in Kansas City with his two dollars for a haircut only to be turned away. But bless him, he waited and the next day the President signed the bill and as soon as he did, there was Gene back at the barbershop and this time he got in the chair. He knew his rights. Thus the history of the Negroes in America—Sojourner Truth to Gene Young.

The Negro riots in the North

WHEN THE riots erupted in Harlem, Brooklyn, Rochester and Jersey City there was anguish and bewilderment; anguish because of the breakdown of law and order, bewilderment because the broadest Civil Rights Bill since the Emancipation Proclamation had just been passed.

In fact, many commentators tied the riots to the passing of the Bill, reasoning that the inflammation broke out when Negroes realized the Rights Bill would not solve their problems. In retrospect, however, I think we can say the riots were in no way connected with the Bill and its passage.

The riots were not race riots. A race riot is one in which both white and Negro communities are actively engaged in retaliation. The Negroes were rioting but I do not think they were even rioting against the cops. They were rioting against frustration. They were rioting against joblessness, against squalid living conditions, against the lack of opportunity.

The Southern segregationists are whistling in the dark when they point to the riots in the North to justify their own attitudes. The Negroes in the North are rioting in an attempt to break into the American middle class and share in some of its wonders; the Negroes in the South are engaged in a wholly different struggle—they are struggling for the recognition of their humanity, to become citizens in the first place.

But it is true the riots mean more than any of this philosophy. There were hoodlums who began a week-long looting holiday; there were Communists, and there were racists who assumed positions of power for as long as the riots lasted, spurring the people on with inflammatory epithets.

I have heard the argument in a thousand places how the

Poles, the Jews, the Irish, the Italians, and the others broke into the middle class without either FEPC or riots. The other immigrants broke in in days when everything was made by hand, when the labor market constantly expanded and all a man really needed was the will to work because there was work somewhere. It wasn't easy. Labor was exploited, underpaid, and millions died young, but automation and a diminishing labor market did not rob those earlier immigrants of hope. Today, even janitorial services are a science and it takes two months of training to teach a man and train him in the use of rather complex janitorial equipment.

And more to the point, the Negro cannot overcome color. The Negro excites emotion, it may be love or hate, pity or contempt, but that emotion rises as soon as we see him. There is nothing he can do about it nor can we. He does not have the advantage that all of us had—the opportunity for at least some degree of anonymity.

And because of his color, the white community forced social and economic compulsions which have prevented the Negro from getting out of the ghetto. We kept him locked in the Harlems of the North at a time when the industrial revolution was at its height and the opportunity for wealth graced our land. And thus the Negro riots at the frustration in living marginally, on the periphery of the richest country in history.

Mayor Thomas J. Whelan of Jersey City accurately and profoundly analyzed the riots when he told reporters that Jersey City had been suffering from a shrinkage of industry, a scattering of middle-class residents into the suburbs and an influx of lower-income people into the city proper. Without federal aid, he said, the city cannot renew itself and if it cannot renew itself it cannot come to the aid of the Negro community. Jersey City has a borrowing capacity of nine million dollars. "We cannot hope to solve this problem with nine million," said Whelan, "any more than Grand Coulee Dam could have been built by the people who lived in that area."

"Walter Lippmann was born smart"

CARL SANDBURG says, "Walter Lippmann was born smart." Mr. Lippmann had written the Introduction to Carl Sandburg's book, "The Chicago Race Riots." And this is what Mr. Lippmann wrote in the year 1919:

> "We shall have to work out with the Negro a relationship which gives him complete access to all the machinery of our common civilization, and yet allows him to live so that no Negro need dream of a white heaven and of bleached angels. Pride of race will come to the Negro when a dark skin is no longer associated with poverty, ignorance, misery, terror, and insult. When this pride arises every white man in America will be the happier for it. He will be able then, as he is not now, to enjoy the finest quality of civilized living—the fellowship of different men."

You can learn a good deal about Mr. Lippmann by again reading *U. S. Foreign Policy: Shield of the Republic,* published in the early 1940's:

> "I have been troubled because of the advantages of hindsight, I am criticizing others for holding views which at the time I may myself have shared, or for a lack of foresight of which I was guilty.

"I did not have the sense to see that the acquisition of the German islands in the Pacific north of the equator by Japan was a fatal blow to our defenses in the Pacific, and I was too weak-minded to take a stand against the exorbitant folly of the Washington Disarmament Conference. In fact I followed the fashion and in editorials for the old New York *World* celebrated the disaster as a triumph and denounced the admirals who dared to protest.

"Of that episode in my life I am ashamed, all the more so because I had no excuse for not knowing better."

Carl Sandburg says, "Walter Lippmann was born smart," to which I would like to add a phrase of my own, with as much finality to it as I can muster: "Walter Lippmann is a man you can trust."

Police work in Camden

MR. GUY HUTCHINS, an accomplished musician, was the director of the Charlotte Symphony. A few years ago he spent a few weeks in Camden, South Carolina. He was teaching a class. One day, out of the blue, Mr. Hutchins told his students how nice it would be if a few Negro high school kids could sit in on the classes. On his way back to Charlotte a few days later, Mr. Hutchins' car was stopped and four white men beat him within an inch of his life. Mr. Hutchins fortunately survived. The story made the front pages in New York, Chicago, Los Angeles, and Philadelphia. One of these big-city reporters asked the Camden Police Chief what action he was taking in the matter. The Chief replied: "I got investigators working around the clock. I myself have gone over every inch

of this town, visiting the merchants and everybody else trying to find out if Hutchins really said that."

The thirsty gamble

IN LITTLE ROCK, Arkansas, there is an eight-storied
four-hundred-bed Catholic hospital. On the fourth floor is the
surgical ward and it is here that Negro patients are also tended
to, although they are in a small majority.

On each and every floor there is a drinking fountain, but on
the fourth floor there are two, neither with a sign but obviously
separate for white and Negro patients.

The hospital administrator says the lack of distinction as to
which is the white and which the colored fountain has proved
an ideal solution. The whites take it for granted that the signs
WHITE and COLORED have been mislaid, and the colored patients do not take offense because the water outlets are truly
equal.

A surgeon at the hospital told me he takes a great delight in
watching a thirsty white pause before these fountains wonder-
ing which one to drink from. When his thirst asserts itself, he
stoops to the nearest one. I recommend this hospital hang a
sign on both fountains reading IF YOU ARE THIRSTY—TAKE A
CHANCE.

My plumber tells me that the average cost for running a
duplicate set of pipes to an ordinary water fountain only to the
first floor of a public building is $268.18. Multiply this by eight
stories by fifty thousand public buildings by twelve Southern
states; and in plumbing alone, the American public, if they cut
out segregation, could wipe out the national debt. We haven't

even touched on the cost of duplicate toilets in all these thouands of buildings, concert halls, and gas stations.

Subtleties of segregation

"LET THE Negroes prove themselves first" is one of the cries raised by the racial segregationists.

I have no disposition to deny or modify the statistics which indicate greater crime proportionately among Negroes than among whites. But it is also true that Negroes are often arrested for infractions and violations which beget only a warning for whites. This factor helps in some degree to account for the statistics which are argued by racists. Often the racist is so busy reading these statistics he doesn't even notice the illogic of his pronouncements. One of the factors he never mentions is that there are virtually no provisions in his home state for demented Negroes.

Not long ago here in Charlotte, a man entered a bar and stepped on the newly polished shoes of another. The man with the shoes was demented. He had a long history of antisocial aberrations. This time he drew a shiv from his coat and stuck it between the ribs of a man innocent of hostility and in the process of apologizing. Multiply this madman by a thousand and you will realize a significant amount of Negro crime is committed by persons who should have been institutionalized long ago.

It is hard enough here in the South to provide adequate facilities for demented whites. For the Negro in North Carolina there is one state institution that cannot even keep up with the demands made by the local inhabitants, let alone the demands made by one-third of the population of the state.

There are areas in the South where respectable Negroes live in fear not only of the white man, but of the itinerant Negro criminal, for the law is slow and bored when it has to test crime or civil suits involving two Negroes.

Southern courts have handed out two-year sentences to Negroes convicted of murder. When the murder is that of another Negro, the court finds the whole thing rather humorous.

I shall even grant that full integration in the public schools might lower the educational standards for a time at least. But to deny equality on any of these grounds is not only a specious argument but a wicked argument, for it employs the *results* of racial segregation as an excuse to perpetuate it.

Similar arguments have been marshaled against all other minorities. They have always been defeated because once equality is granted, the statistics soon become proportional statistics.

Proof of individual worth is something each of us must earn by individual effort. But it is impossible to take "potluck" with the rest of the population unless you, too, can move about as a free citizen; unless you, too, can have the benefit of all the facilities and institutions established by society.

The most remarkable thing about the integration controversy is that despite the progress, such as it is, no one, north, south, east, or west, has given an inch except under the pressure of law. The courts alone enforce integration and without the courts there would be no movement at all.

Even with the aid and support of the courts, it is hard to achieve advances. This is because there are areas of segregation which even the law cannot touch. These areas are both subtle and impregnable and the segregationists hide behind these barricades and fire away.

The school board never quite surrenders to the court order. When Negro parents apply for their child's transfer to a previous "all white" school because they, the Negroes, live only a block away, the school board first says, "Come back Tuesday," and on Tuesday it says, "The blank is incorrectly filled out." The board then insists on an oral examination of each Negro child and one of the questions is: "Aren't you happy in your *own* [Negro] school?" (which is eight miles away). Now I submit this last is a question Plato might answer orally and without hesitation, but not a ten-year-old child.

When the community hospital accepts Hill-Burton funds from the United States Government, the hospital must agree that its services and facilities are open to all, regardless of race, creed, or color. Complaints on segregation bring a government investigating team to see if indeed Negroes must continue using the inadequate and sometimes inhumane facilities set aside for them.

The investigating team finds this is so, but no one can put his finger on a violation of the agreement with the Government. The hospital authorities say they would gladly take Negroes as patients—if they applied for admission.

Now why don't Negroes apply for admission? Because a patient must be admitted to the hospital by a doctor affiliated with the staff. There are no Negro doctors on the staff of the hospital, not even a hospital which was built with government money. The hospital authorities protest they are not discriminating against Negro physicians, surgeons, and dentists; it is simply that the Negroes cannot qualify for the staff because one of the requirements is membership in the state medical associaton. In most Southern states no Negro can become a member of the state medical (or dental) association because the state law forbids this integration.

The authorities convince the investigating team: "We are not discriminatory. Let a Negro become a member of the state medical (or dental) association and he can admit what patients he wishes."

All of which means that Negroes must continue to take their inferior health services.

What we need to "investigate" next is why the Negro infant mortality rate is five times that of the "white" infant mortality rate.

Senator Sam Ervin of my state of North Carolina is a man of warmth and a fine sense of humor. He is the best storyteller in the Congress since the days of Alben Barkley.

In a Senate filibuster against the late President Kennedy's proposal to extend voting rights to all those who have finished six years of schooling, Senator Ervin asked: "Show me where the voting rights of a single Negro have been violated in North Carolina."

It is indeed difficult to prove violations of voting rights, and even if there is a clear-cut violation, it is a difficult task for a Negro sharecropper or janitor to file a protest and institute the legal process to have his voting rights restored.

But we know for a fact that Negroes do not vote in many of the counties and districts of the Deep South, and one of the reasons they do not vote is because in some way their rights are denied them. Here is one of the methods used:

In a North Carolina rural precinct a Negro arrives to register and the registrar says gently, "Jim, you don't want to be the first Negro to register, do you? Why not let a bunch of others register first? It will look better that way." Jim sees the wisdom of this suggestion and out he goes and the registrar says the same thing to each Negro, male or female.

Now, say, a group of Negroes band together to register jointly. The registrar still has recourse to deny them their rights. Most of the Negroes in Mississippi, Alabama, and Louisiana are farmers and they have to select a day that is mutually convenient. One farmer provides the transportation and he goes about the countryside picking up the others. It is easy to alert the registrar to this, that a truck filled with twenty-six Negroes who want to register is approaching town. The registrar puts a sign on his door. CLOSED FOR THE DAY. It is not easy for sharecroppers and small farmers to keep coming back. It is in truth a large effort, consuming considerable time and risk.

In one district in Alabama when a Negro was able to answer the formal question on the literacy test, the registrar asked new questions such as, "Tell me the name of the Sheriff of Shmendrick County." And, finally, and so help me, the voter was asked, "How many bubbles in a bar of soap?"

In Selma, Alabama, last year, hundreds of Negroes ran a gauntlet of armed state troopers and stood in line eight hours without food or water in an attempt to register.

In Fayette County, Tennessee, Negroes who registered suffered serious economic retaliation. "Many Negroes lost their jobs," the Civil Rights Commission reported. "A list of the 'culprits' was circulated. White merchants quite trading with them. Pressure was brought to prevent suppliers in Memphis from selling to them. Their credit was stopped; their loans recalled; their mortgages foreclosed. They could not buy the necessities of life. One white banker was quoted as saying, "My secretary's got the names of the three hundred twenty-five who registered. I tell them, anybody on that list, no need coming into this bank. He'll get no crop loans here. Every store has got that list!"

Committee of one

WHILE I'm convinced anti-Semitism is a constant of Western culture and incurable, I'm always intrigued with the possible plans to make it immobile.

Will anti-Semitism continue?

Perhaps not in the form we have known it in Europe since the Middle Ages.

If it is a *constant* of Western Civilization as I believe it is, how deep is it? In a peaceful, democratic society, how far beneath the surface does it lurk?

I am no Jeremiah, coming along with a cure for a disease that has plagued us for two thousand years. What I suggest is that my cure may work because of the specific set of circumstances in a specific place—the United States of America, in the mid-twentieth century.

I propose for American Jewry that it dedicate all its social-action societies, fraternities, rabbinical assemblies and charities to the single cause of civil rights and that Jews fight for everyone who needs help except themselves.

Thus the chalk mark on the sidewalk or the mud thrown at a temple would become a huge joke. We would laugh at it. The psychopaths who did this would become so frustrated at our laughter they would jump off the nearest pier.

When you fight for others you build an impregnable wall of security around yourself. We should turn all our energies and our finances, and all our trained personnel and our trained legal departments, to fight for Gentiles who are in trouble; the Negroes, the migratory workers, the Mexican wetbacks, and thousands of individuals everywhere who may need our help.

Wherever there's an authentic problem of civil rights, a Jewish lawyer should be there within twenty-four hours.

I mentioned this in New Orleans after the Supreme Court decision ending racial segregation in the public schools in 1954. I told a convention of Jewish leaders that for the first time in two thousand years we Jews had an opportunity to fight for democracy when we ourselves were not the target. Up to now, whenever we have fought for human rights, we were the ones on the firing line. But now there was an opportunity for us to turn over the entire Jewish establishment to help the Negro in his fight so that he could remove forever from this civilization the concept of a second-class citizenship.

I think if we followed this course, we would have struck the first major blow against anti-Semitism. The silver miners in Peru, the Eskimos in Alaska, and millions of people in the villages and towns of Asia and Africa would hear of it, and millions of people throughout the world would be uplifted. A new optimism would wash over them in wonder that the community of six million Jews of America had constituted themselves into a *committee of one* for the sole purpose of preserving the Christian ethic.

Atlanta's achievement

ATLANTA, GEORGIA, was the spiritual capital of the Confederacy. It was the city Sherman burned, the city whose fall signaled the end of the Confederacy.

It is the capital of Georgia, the state which gave birth to the modern Ku Klux Klan and to a series of racist philosophers from Tom Watson to Marvin Griffin.

When people talked about the end of enforced segregation they always whispered the name Atlanta; that the Georgia capital would be the last city to accept the change. It was the last bastion, or so we all thought.

Yet Atlanta proved itself the most modern and perhaps the most moral of all Southern cities. Reason fled Little Rock, Montgomery, Jackson, and Birmingham, but reason has a home in Atlanta. When integration came to Atlanta no mobs roamed its streets, none of its schools closed. It was the first American city to seek reapportionment in order to deal with its problems equitably on the basis of majority rule.

And I suspect the difference between Atlanta and Birmingham this day is that Atlanta has Ralph McGill and Birmingham has "Bull" Connor. The one is a leader and the other is a simple intransigent.

Mayor Hartsfield of Atlanta and his successor, Mayor Allen and the present Governor Sanders and Lillian Smith and others have helped set the face of Georgia toward the truly New South, one which Senator Richard Russell would not recognize.

When the Supreme Court ordered the desegregation of the public schools in 1954, a silence settled over the South. It was neither ominous nor threatening. It was a bewildering silence. One governor explained this silence. He said that the people were seething underneath.

No one was "seething" really. Those who were silent were waiting for their leaders to point the way. And where the leadership did not materialize, the White Citizens' Councils filled the vacuum. It is as simple as that.

The Ralph McGills are a good sign. They prove we are not yet ready to have all our problems settled by a computer ma-

chine. It proves that the best response is still generated by the
courageous morality of individuals.

Negro anti-Semites

I HAVE heard a disturbing question raised from the audience in recent months.

"How come you speak so strongly for Negro integration,
Mr. Golden? Don't you know there are Negro anti-Semites?"

This is a puzzling attitude, one that dismays me. Assuming
the truth of some Negro anti-Semitism, it is minimal compared to the other forms of this virulent prejudice. Why do the
folks think democracy is a matter of you-scratch-my-back-and-
I'll-scratch-yours?

The Negroes are people, not paragons. As people they have
the same faults, vices, fears and are as badly informed as anybody else. Negroes have their share of greed, avarice, hatred,
and ignorance. But they have the same virtues, or potential
virtues, as humanity everywhere.

I do not doubt there are Negro anti-Semites. Negroes so
afflicted are like children who don't get the point of the joke
but who laugh because the adults are laughing. They are like
the Copts in the Middle East who imitated the walk of the
French officers.

Neither Negro anti-Semitism nor any Negro vices bear on
the important subject of civil rights for all.

My own experience tells me a Negro anti-Semite is about as
convincing as a Jewish white supremacist (and indeed we do
have Jewish white supremacists): both think they can become
French officers by merely imitating the walk.

Integration: $150,000 per man

I MADE a speech at the Methodist Pfeiffer College in Misenheimer, North Carolina.

The students at Pfeiffer gave me a generous reception as well as their generous attention.

Pfeiffer is a particularly impressive place. Its campus is easily one of the most beautiful in the country. Eight hundred and fifty students are in attenance at the school and all seem imbued with the single aim of getting an education.

I am always a reporter and while I was at Pfeiffer I came up with the important story of how much integration cost the school.

When Pfeiffer integrated (long before the public schools adopted their token integration), it decided there would be no publicity about the matter. It asked the wire services not to run the story since it would make things easier for all concerned, and the AP and the UPI agreed. So the college accepted a Negro and rented him the usual accommodations in the student dormitory shortly after the Supreme Court decision which outlawed segregation.

This small college was just completing a necessary building fund campaign and it collected pledges amounting to eight hundred and fifty thousand dollars. Word got out that a Negro was living in one of the halls and pretty soon one hundred and fifty thousand dollars of the eight hundred and fifty thousand dollars was canceled.

The officials of the college visited those who had canceled their pledges in order to explain the reasons for Pfeiffer's step but to no avail. So it cost Pfeiffer that much at least to integrate one man. The college, however, neither regrets its decision nor did it ever waver.

The college pays in other ways, too. Some years ago there was a great water shortage in Pfeiffer and to prevent a recurrence of this inconvenience the school arranged to build a water pipeline to its campus. But it took two years for the City of Albemarle to grant its approval for running this line from its water supply although it is adequate for a city five times the present size.

These annoyances are subtle and no one has said openly we don't like you because you've integrated, but the frustrations are there.

As if Pfeiffer didn't have enough troubles, it invited me there only a month after the late Senator Estes Kefauver had paid a visit and from one of the big millowners came a telegram saying:

INVITING HARRY GOLDEN ON TOP OF SENATOR KEFAUVER IS
THE LAST STRAW.

No place to roost

A MEMBER of the Air Force, Raymond M. Bacon, advises me that housing at the air base in Vandenberg, California, is denied to Negroes. Mr. Bacon, himself a Negro, contacted all the other Negroes at the Vandenberg Air Force Base and found that the story was the same. All found it impossible to let vacant apartments, all feel they have been denied accommodations because they are Negroes.

Airman Bacon did a thorough job calling all the rental

agents in the Santa Maria-Lompac, California, area who had a listing in the Central Telephone Company directory. These agents received the airman enthusiastically over the telephone. When Bacon approached personally, the managers explained candidly that they would not rent to him or to any other Negro.

Raymond Bacon is an airman third class, with no outside income but his Air Force pay. To keep down expenses, he resigned himself to calling the realtors, and after ascertaining that there were apartments available, asking them honestly over the telephone whether they would rent to him, a Negro. They all told him just as honestly that they could not let him have an apartment and keep their white tenants.

Another Negro airman first class sent me a copy of a letter he wrote his commander in which he said, "I have tried to rent a place for my family by the month. Even where I was willing to go to one hundred dollars, which I can hardly afford to pay, I was turned down because they will not rent to a Negro."

That these Negro airmen are willing to present this correspondence and have their names used and publicized is evidence enough how desperate is this situation at the Vandenberg Air Force Base at Vandenberg, California.

What fatal inhibition immobilizes the base commander?

What country do these realtors think Negro airmen serve?

Who pays the highest rent?

THE ANSWER is easy. The Negro pays the highest rent and pays equally the highest price for realty.

The resistance in keeping Negroes out of better neighborhoods is not, as has been alleged, to keep realty values stable, but rather to keep realty values elsewhere inflated.

Let me offer a concrete example. I made an inquiry at a duplex (two-family home) in one of Charlotte's slum areas. Four Negro families lived in this run-down house, each paying fifteen-dollars-a-week rent. Their aggregate monthly rent was therefore around two hundred forty dollars, which is about fifty dollars more than a beautiful brick duplex in one of the city's best neighborhoods brings in aggregate. Any reader can make the same investigation in his or her city and come close to the same result.

My father always said we poor paid more for coal than J. P. Morgan. Of course, in those days everybody blamed everything on J. P. Morgan. Nevertheless, my father was right. We bought coal for our tenement in one-hundred-pound bags which meant we paid about eighteen dollars a ton. J. P. Morgan presumably bought coal by the ton, which then was selling for about four dollars and fifty cents.

Sterilization in Mississippi

GOVERNOR PAUL B. JOHNSON of Mississippi, he of the tempered approach to serious problems, has just signed a bill which makes the parents of a second illegitimate child guilty of a misdemeanor. The bill permits these parents to escape penalties by undergoing voluntary sterilization. Without sterilization, parents face up to ninety days in jail and two hundred and fifty dollars in fines for the first violation and up to six months and five hundred dollars for subsequent violations.

Mississippi, which cherishes its image as a state filled with

Christian charity and goodwill, insists the bill is designed to curb illegitimacy and reduce the welfare rolls.

It might be well to point out to the God-fearing Mississippi legislators and Governor that people do not have illegitimate children in order to collect welfare. To argue that they do would be to argue that the women of Biblical times had illegitimate children in order to be stoned to death.

What I think important is Mississippi's motives. Just how does it intend to enforce this bill? I can see it has the jails in which to incarcerate mothers and I can even see the judges who will enforce these penalties, but where will they collect the doctors who will perform sterilization? God knows, I have little patience with the American Medical Association and its stubbornness on the subject of national medical insurance, but not for a second do I believe it will sanction doctors who sterilize the parents (providing the State can locate *both* parents, another problem) who are under duress from the courts. We are barely two decades from the horror of the Nazi massacres and yet an American state is leading the way back. The infirm and the retarded and the racially suspect women are dragged screaming to the block because the Nazi State had proclaimed them unfit to be mothers. Now Mississippi has also made up its mind who should and who should not bear children.

Is Mississippi really interested in cutting its welfare rolls? Not really. The bulk of Mississippi's welfare money doesn't come from Mississippi; it comes from the Federal Government, from the taxpayers in Michigan, Connecticut, and Ohio.

In fact, the bill and its passage reveals one of the obvious Southern cruelties. The bill is basically an anti-Negro bill. The talk about the peace and harmony of the two races in the South has always been a disguise. The bill is a vengeance bill, designed to punish Negroes for sex; conceived and passed because one of the white segregationist's recurrent fantasies is that the Negro enjoys a wider sexual freedom than he. If this is true, it is only because the segregationist has insisted it is true and has conditioned Negroes to its truth.

This is the Southern nightmare and such a bill is the dreamer's vengeance. Does any Northern state ever entertain such proposals? Never. But every Southern state every other year considers such legislation. Only Mississippi so far has had the barbarity to pass such a law.

Do not tell me, therefore, Mississippi is not a police state. Surely there are people who deplore such measures. Anywhere up north or west, a man can pick a good fight discussing birth control. To imagine that a bill like this could receive the Governor's endorsement simply proves no one dares speak out because everyone knows the bill is a punitive measure against Negroes, the white man's revenge for the Negroes' big fun and the myth that eats the white man's heart out.

To be where the people are

THE HOPE for the simple solution is based on error, error that history goes in a straight line without twisting and turning and yes, perhaps even stopping to decide which direction to take next.

We had no idea in 1776 that we would discover the Mesabi Range in Minnesota; that it would become United States Steel and change the face of America, with new challenges and new ideas; that it would result in the organization of our urban culture and the problems of what to do with our leisure and how to establish new roots in a mobile society.

Those of us over fifty years of age remember when our entire political life revolved around the alderman, the local sheriff, or the county commissioner. We were involved with these officials. It may have meant a job, a license of some kind, or getting a boy out of trouble. To us the world was infinite. England was off some place where King Henry VIII and his wives lived. France meant Joan of Arc or Lafayette.

Today the sheriff and the county commissioner are important, but of equal importance to us is the Prime Minister of Viet Nam.

The simple solution is the one that makes Justice Earl Warren a villain. In some Southern cities as you leave the airport you are greeted with a billboard: IMPEACH EARL WARREN. Justice Earl Warren, they say, destroyed their way of life, but you'll notice they rarely mention Chief Justice Fred M. Vinson, bone-of-the-bone and blood-of-the-blood of the Old South. It was Justice Vinson who struck the first blow. The decision of Justice Vinson in the Sweatt case three years before the Warren Court's decision was monumental. A Negro had applied for entry into the University of Texas Law School. He was denied admittance. He sued. The State of Texas proved in court that the separate Law School for Negroes was a good law school. But Justice Vinson broke the back of racial segregation. His decision should be read in every classroom once a year like the Gettysburg Address. What Justice Vinson declared was that the facilities have nothing to do with it, that segregation of itself, whether it is equal or not equal, is evil, unconstitutional, and immoral; that the process of education involves more than facilities. It involves the classmates, the conversations, the size of the library, the prestige of the faculty and the prestige of the alumni, and, most important of all, the opportunity to exchange ideas with other future lawyers, judges, jurors, prosecuting attorneys, and members of the pardoning board.

It reminds me of a story told to me by Dr. Parrish, an elderly Negro college professor.

Across the years he went once a week to lecture at Hampton up in Washington and he took the overnight train from Atlanta and he bought a lower berth. To maintain racial segregation the railroad always gave a Negro with a Pullman ticket a private room for no extra money. One night, says Dr. Parrish, the conductor felt a little sad about his participation in this humiliating Jim Crow procedure, and he knocked on the door. "Is everything all right, Doctor?" he said, and the conductor came around at least three times during the course of the evening.

"Is everything all right, Doctor?" Finally, Dr. Parrish opened the door and wearily answered, "No, everything is not all right. I want to be where the people are."

The simple solution which you hear now is that "the public accommodations" section of the civil rights legislation is an infringement upon private property.

The "public accommodations" section of the civil rights legislation makes no more an infringement upon private property than the legislation which requires a businessman to buy a license for his store or restaurant, and the legislation which forces him to admit public health authorities to inspect his place of business, and the legislation which demands he get a building permit if he wants to make an addition. The Federal and State governments moreover specify the minimum wage this businessman must pay his employees and they limit the hours he can work them. Both the State and Federal governments require a businessman to collect and remit taxes from both employees and customers.

A law requiring the businessman to be color blind as to the complexion of his customers seems no more an infringement on his freedom of action than any legislation passed to benefit the public weal.

The American Dream is not a puff of smoke. There was a rabbi in Philadelphia in the early part of the nineteenth century. His name was Gershom Seixas. He had seen Washington as a young man and now the rabbi was old and delivering a sermon on the occasion of Lafayette's visit to America nearly fifty years after the signing of the Declaration of Independence. The rabbi referred to America as a miracle, a miracle of God. There were thirty or forty men involved in the founding of America, he said, and each of these men could have been placed in succeeding half-centuries and he would have enriched his time; but there they were, the thirty or forty of them all together, living at the same moment in history, conferring with one another and establishing the American Dream.

And what essentially is the American Dream? What is America? America is not a skyscraper with the moon hanging over it like a FOR RENT sign, and neither is America a feather bed where freedom is snoozing till the cows come home; and neither is America the mountain and the plain and a seaport. America is neither a skyscraper nor geography. America and the American Dream is an Idea. And perhaps an Idea which has had no parallel in human history. Each of us can jot down on a piece of paper his version of the American Dream, and I suspect each version would have validity. I like to think of the American Dream in terms of an Idea which is still one of the wonders of the world, the opportunity to enter the open society on the basis of character, talent, and willingness to participate and to be involved in the common welfare and security. This Idea is uniquely American. Even in sister democracies we find that the economic and social classes are still stratified to a considerable degree. The apprentice to a tailor will become a tailor. The boy who throws the peanuts at the cricket game will grow up to be the foreman of the boys who throw the peanuts at the cricket game. In America we have this tremendous mobility, not only the mobility from place to place, but also from class to class, from neighborhood to neighborhood, and from one income level to another income level.

But this privilege was not handed to them on a silver platter. There were many heartaches and many struggles; because this American Dream needs to be guarded night and day, guarded from those who believe history goes in a straight line and who say, as they have said at many critical moments in our history, "Let us stop the process, let us digest our gains, let us do it later maybe, gradually maybe."

And so there was a time when the Mormons were chased and hounded across the continent and the Catholics had trouble in parts of our country and the Baptists were persecuted, and the First Methodist church in New York was built with a fireplace so that when the sheriff came around, the worshipers could hide their prayer books and pretend that they were merely visiting a friend. But the Philadelphia rabbi was probably right, that America was a miracle because the foundation had given us the strength and the wisdom of that second look, and at each moment of crisis we succeeded in the American Dream of the free entry into the open society of our country.

And we have another such crisis today. Yet the racial crisis that invades the American conscience today invades it at a time when it must be united and ready for the most crucial struggle of its history. Even in President Jefferson's day, with continents remote from each other, and with communication primitive, the author of the Declaration of Independence realized that we must have "a decent respect to the opinions of mankind."

It is not mere rhetoric to affirm the simple but powerful truth of the American Dream and state the question: All our immigrant groups from 1840 to 1920, in the order of their coming, the Germans, the Scandinavians, the Irish, the Jews, the Slavs, the Italians, and the Greeks, found their way into the open society based on individual initiative, talent, ambition, and character; and yet our Negro citizens, sixth-generation Americans mostly, have been forced to fight every step of the way and in both North and South are still denied this mobility of movement which is essentially the American Dream.

And if we look upon it selfishly we must see at once the awesome loss to the American growth of wealth both spiritual and material. Because the newcomer to a society has always provided it with a tremendous vitality.

I have heard it said that our correction of this problem is an action long awaited of us by millions of people around the world. Ralph Waldo Emerson once wrote, "Your manners are always under examination and by committees that little suspect it . . . but are awarding or denying you very high prizes when you least think of it." I'm sure that when we do better in the field of race relations our example will continue to help men everywhere who struggle for freedom, but *what the rest of the world sees and hears us do is not so important as what we see and hear ourselves do and even that is not so important as what God sees and hears us do.*

The true victor

AGAINST the turn toward health and wholeness that will come from the winning of justice, the segregationist struggles unreasoningly. He has not even stopped to consider that if tomorrow he gave the Negro everything he demands—the right to vote, attend school, and compete with his skills in the labor market on a fair basis—the Negro then would only be starting from scratch.

The immediate victor, the real victor, would be the white Southerner. He would be the victor, first, because a great burden would be lifted from him. The white Southerner would be able to go about his own business for the first time in more than a century.

The white Southerner would be able to move back into what was once the most politically creative society in the Western Hemisphere, the society that produced Washington, Jefferson, Mason, Pinckney, and hosts of other great minds. Today, Southern leaders such as Senator J. William Fulbright of Arkansas and Senator Richard Russell of Georgia and Senator Lister Hill of Alabama, men unusually gifted, have enslaved and handicapped themselves—no less than the Negro—because they have had to worry about whether Negroes were moving from the back of the bus to the front, thereby enraging their white constituents.

The great paradox here is that the Southerner thinks of himself as a fiscal conservative. He wants the budget balanced and in recent years he has hung the picture of Senator Harry Byrd of Virginia in the space once occupied by William Jennings Bryan.

Yet this fiscal conservative, with the lowest per capita earnings in the land, has wasted his meager resources in trying to maintain facilities and whole systems in duplicate, for "white" and for "colored," down to the two sets of unnecessary plumbing fixtures for the segregated toilets in the courthouse. The waste of money has been so fantastic that much of it is hidden from view. If the Southern segregationist shows any shame at all about maintaining the racial status quo, it is in hiding some of the ridiculous cost of racial segregation.

The victory of the white Southerner will be so overwhelming he will eventually agree with Negro Dr. Albert Dent, president of Dillard University in New Orleans, who has said that one day, in retrospect, the white Southerner will look back upon the Supreme Court decisions favoring desegregation as the beginning of his own emancipation.

He will finally put the racists' classic question directly to his sister—and she'll laugh right in his face. She's been wise to him all along. The Negro seeks not white women but simply the right to be master of his own house. The Negro culture has been a matriarchy. The wages of the female domestic have been fairly steady, while the Negro male has been victimized when the financial stability of the community was in the slightest danger. The Negro male is therefore an itinerant, more or less, and he, like his children, is dependent on the money his wife and daughters bring home.

The German poet Heinrich Heine warned his fellow Jews in the middle of the nineteenth century, "We must be twice as good to get half as much."

This will be the hard truth the Negroes will have to face, in the North as well as in the South. The Negro's entry into the open society as a political and economic equal will not bring him automatic ease and relaxation but automatic hard work and struggle. The Negro for the next two decades will be poorly educated, poorly informed, and poorly trained even if everything he asks is granted tomorrow by Congress.

By instinct, Negroes know the way to reduce these odds is first by education, and it is for the prospects of equal education he has made his boldest, strongest, and most sustained moves.

The segregationist women

THE white segregationist who works so hard protecting Southern Womanhood has a singularly thankless job. So few Southern women thank him. In fact, the segregationist cause has curiously failed to provide an articulate woman spokesman. I do not mean they have not provided their own Eleanor Roosevelt—this they aren't going to do. The wartime Republicans produced a Clare Booth Luce who gave the language such expressions as "globaloney" and "G.I. Jim" and who almost succumbed some years later to poisoned paint clumsily applied by Italian workmen to the ceiling of her villa where she was serving as Ambassadress. Nor have the segregationists produced an Oveta Culp Hobby as have the Eisenhower Republicans. Mrs. George C. Wallace's public comments indicate only pride in her husband, and I have yet to hear from Mrs. Orval C. Faubus. If Senator Eastland's wife has any thoughts on the separation of the races, she keeps them to herself.

Yet the civil rights advocates have produced a Gloria Richardson in Maryland and Gloria Baker Motley of the N.A.A.C.P.'s Legal Defense Fund, and a Septima Poinsette Clark.

The segregationist can point to the shouting women mobbed around the Little Rock Central High School and it is true that one of them screamed, "My God, they're letting the niggers in!" It is true that the segregationist can collect women to shout. It is strange that he cannot produce articulation.

In fact, Southern women who are articulate tend to despise segregation. I sometimes suspect their intelligence and forthrightness is inspired by their recognition of injustice. On the record, the Southern woman is absolutely unconcerned about "mongrelization." She doesn't even think about it. She only thinks and writes about how cruel and misguided the Southern male is likely to get considering the Negro.

A century ago, Mary Boykin Chesnut, the wife of one of Jefferson Davis's Cabinet members, wrote, "Under slavery we live surrounded by prostitutes, yet an abandoned woman is sent out of any decent house. Who thinks any worse of a Negro or mulatto woman for being a thing we can't name? God forgive us, but ours is a monstrous system, a wrong and an inequity!"

It was a Georgia girl, Lillian Smith, who, with her friend Paula Snelling, edited the first antisegregation publication below the Mason-Dixon line. If anyone can be said to have "discovered" the Negro writers of our country, it was she and Miss Snelling in *South Today*.

I have seen on Confederate Memorial Day and in the heat of a political campaign the wives of Southern politicians look with shame and embarrassment at husbands promising to defend the home, wife and daughter against the nonexisting sexual incursions of the Negro. The ladies indeed look as if they want to disappear from that platform. In the open society, they have promised chastity, virtue, and faithfulness, and the husbands are prophesying that if the State grants Negroes their constitutional rights all of this goes out the window.

For the blind

ITEM in the *Church News*, Houston Chronicle Publishing Company, Houston, Texas, July 18, 1963:

A chartered bus will take the blind people to Waco

August 23rd through August 25th for the Texas Church
Conference for the Blind.

There will be no charges for the bus—only $10.00
per person for the six (6) meals and two nights' lodging.
All who are interested in going please get in touch with
Mrs. Bromie Hollon, OX 5-3390. *White race only.*

Believing is seeing

THE prejudiced man tends to see what he wants to see.
Thus if he believes that the Jews want to "take over," he will
see every Jew as "shrewd," "crafty," and all the other "virtues"
along this line; he will see the Negro as "sexy" and refer to
every Negro male (sight unseen) as that "big buck nigra,"
including those who are no bigger than jockeys and have tuberculosis to boot. (In the South, tuberculosis is fourteenth as a
cause of death among whites and second as a cause of death
among Negroes.)

What happened to Leonard Goldstein?

A LOCAL Internal Revenue man with whom I have a
nodding acquaintance stopped me the other day and asked me
quite seriously: "Mr. Golden, do you know what happened to
Leonard Goldstein?" Now I am probably one of the most
articulate little fat guys in existence, but I just stood there like
a dope. He followed it up, "Leonard Goldstein, a Jewish fellow; used to run such-and-such mercantile company, incorpo-
rated." After a torturous delay I finally came up with, "I never
heard of the guy." At that moment I doubt whether there was

a more unconvinced human being on this earth than my Internal friend. He no more believed me than if I had suddenly said that I had never heard of Pericles ("That's two Jews he never heard of").

It never ceases to intrigue me how so many non-Jews believe that all the Jews meet in some cellar once a week—Baruch, Frankfurter, Danny Kaye, Einstein, Eddie Cantor, and all the rest of us.

Ah, if we only had some of the qualities with which we are reproached! "Sticking together," for instance. Is there a more noble thought that could come from the mind of man? How I wish it were true, or at least five-percent true.

Coming back to "Leonard Goldstein," the reason I had never heard of him is probably because he was not interested in the Shakespeare lectures I delivered around Charlotte, or in the communal affairs of the city and the state and its institutions, all of which interest me very much. On a broad basis, people make their contacts on a basis of a common interest or a common devotion to an idea or a project. If, for instance, columnist David Lawrence, a Jew, and Dr. Martin Luther King, Jr., a Negro Christian clergyman, were with me in a canoe and suddenly the thing hit an iceberg—being a little fat guy I could only save one of them—whom do you think I would save? Come to think of it, the idea deserves a drink right now. And I might add, David Lawrence would probably save Dr. King too. Wouldn't he?

The joys of Alabama

THE University of Alabama offers both extension and television courses. While it would be hard for Alabama University to segregate its audience into white and Negro for either of these two courses, it is still done. In order to get university credit for either, you have to submit an application with a picture of yourself. If you do not send a picture you must state whether you are white or Negro. Only whites qualify for credits. Since the Golden Vertical Negro Plan, based on the observation that the races mingle without incident in public places where there are no seats, has worked so well throughout the South, I suggest that Negroes promise on their application to stand up while the televised French class of the University of Alabama is on the air.

Learning at long distance

IN THE Blue Ridge mountains of western North Carolina thirteen Negro students ride more than one hundred miles to school every day. They go to a high school in a different county because there are no separate high schools for Negroes in their own.

While this county does have two schools and enough vacant seats to accommodate the thirteen Negro students, the humanitarian school board still feels it is worth the money to the taxpayers and the degradation to the students to perpetuate this arrangement.

In nearby Avery County there is a Negro high school which has one teacher and six students. That is the only Negro high school. Avery County has three "white" schools, the smallest of which lists eight teachers. It would seem that combining any one "white" high school and the Negro high school would result in a more efficient educational process. It is not to be.

Teddy's stand

THEODORE ROOSEVELT said, "States' rights should be
preserved when they mean people's rights, not when they
mean people's wrongs."

I wonder why the ultraconservatives aren't out gunning for
the first Mr. Roosevelt.

We all look like Davy Crockett

DECLAN HAUN is one of the best news photographers.
He made the pictures for a *Saturday Evening Post* story on
the Presidential campaign of Governor George C. Wallace of
Alabama. The photographer stuck pretty close to the segrega-
tionist-politician, and during a relaxed moment Haun told
Wallace that he had once lived in the South and was familiar
with racial segregation, but that he now lived in a Chicago
apartment house with a dozen Negro families and he, his wife,
and his children were perfectly at ease and enjoy the fellowship.

The next morning at breakfast, the Alabama Governor said,
"Haun, I can see why you are happy in Chicago with Negro
neighbors—it's because you're Jewish."

Declan Haun merely smiled. He's as Irish as Jim Farley,
Bobby Kennedy, and James Cagney.

The happy impostor

HENRY SIMMONS was a shy middle-aged bachelor of Anglo-Saxon descent, and assistant production manager at United Products Corporation.

He didn't drive a car partly because he enjoyed riding in Sam Cohen's taxicab. Sam was jolly, improvident, and a great talker. Henry listened to Sam's accounts of his joys and sorrows, and felt a great liking and sympathy for Sam.

The office had a few characters who were always making derogatory remarks about Jews. It irked Henry Simmons and one day, thinking of his common humanity with Sam Cohen, he looked up from his desk and quietly said, "Just what have you fellows got against us?" Complete silence about Jews prevailed and as word got around that Henry was Jewish, he got notices of all the charity drives, and cheerfully sent his checks and became known as a very kind and charitable Jew.

This has been going on for several years and Henry knows no one would ever believe him if he said he wasn't a Jew, never even remotely had been a Jew. There is only one thought on Henry's mind. Is he too old, at forty-eight, to make his *bar mitzvah?*

Interracial gesture

IN THE men's room of the Hoke County (North Carolina) Courthouse there are three stalls, marked, WHITE, COLORED, INDIAN. However, there is only one urinal.

The end of caste?

IT HAPPENED a few days before President Lyndon Johnson signed the Civil Rights Act which the late President Kennedy had sent to the Congress early in 1963.

We were amazed and breathless when we saw two white
women charging a third who had been parading with Negro
demonstrators in St. Augustine, Florida. They held her to the
ground and with their feet these two women, beyond imagin-
ing, stomped her. Can Negroes swimming in the ocean inspire
such violence? What made these two ordinary women deny
their femininity and their civilization?

And we held our breath when we learned that three civil
rights workers were missing outside Philadelphia, Mississippi.
They were young men, boys just out of college or just ready to
be graduated. The F.B.I. investigated and the President sent
Allen Dulles to confer with Mississippi's governor, Paul Johnson.

At the time I said it would be extremely doubtful if they
ever found the bodies of those three young men. This crime
was committed by experienced people who knew the swamp-
lands of Mississippi. They knew how to commit a crime "without a trace." They have had long experience. It was not a
unique aberration.

As we mourn for the three boys we should remember that
hundreds upon hundreds of Negroes have disappeared, and
disappeared without an obituary or a mourner to sorrow for
their death. They had bested a white man in a cotton deal or
they had tried to register to vote, or they had brought a lawsuit
against a store for redress of grievance and then the men came
and dragged them from their shacks and beat them and tossed

their dead bodies into the swamps or the woodlands. Then the sheriff came and he sternly asked the Negro mother: "Where's your Jim? He owes eight dollars back taxes." This was the usual covering operation. It happened just that way a thousand times. More than a thousand times.

And the woman cowered, clutching her children, and the sheriff surmised, "Ran off to Chicago with that woman, didn't he? That's what they all do." The woman understood. She knew that is what will go into the record and there was nothing she could do about it.

Now it is manifestly absurd to believe the segregationists were charging Negro swimmers to protect the Atlantic Ocean from contamination; it is equally absurd to believe that a lynch mob grabbed three boys from a station wagon to protect the Greek, Jewish, Chinese, and Yankee hotel syndicate restaurants that form the vast majority of the eating establishments of the South.

No, neither restaurants nor oceans spurred the mobs. The segregationists know what has been at stake all these years since 1954. White supremacy was at stake. And white supremacy was a wealth that could never be dissipated. A man could lose his money, he could lose his farm, but once upon a time he was always superior no matter what cotton prices were. He handed down this superiority to his son and to his family. He has fought for white supremacy as monarchs once fought to protect the divine right of kings.

The segregationist has been so blinded by this threat to his supremacy he even believed for a while he could claim support from the North. But the Negro struggle in the North, the backlash so called, was centered on realty values and job displacement and annoyance.

The Negro in the North was trying to move into the middle class. In the South, he was trying to move into life itself. And once he moved into life, the segregationist knew perforce the mainstream will eventually sweep him along. And white superiority will drown.

Southern segregation was a caste system, and nothing more. Caste systems are notorious not for promising that life will be better but for promising that caste itself will blur misfortune.

PART 3

The D.A.R. and the U.N.

Liberals and conservatives

MAN's first cry is a protest against discomfort at being dislodged from his snug security, and a lively fear of the future. To retreat is instinctive, and is counterbalanced by curiosity and hope. There is no way back and the liberals know this. Mankind is going forward into a totally unknown future and will try to provide implementation for a new and better day. There will be a tremendous breach between liberals and conservatives, each reflecting one side of man's nature.

Lyndon B. Johnson

JOHN F. KENNEDY's finest achievement was Lyndon B. Johnson. There were a dozen men Kennedy might sooner have picked for his running mate, but he picked Johnson. There were a dozen reasons why Johnson could have refused the second spot but he said yes. A monumental tragedy and a lucky chance gave us Lyndon B. Johnson for our thirty-sixth President. Yet there is a certain justice in it.

Kennedy was the first man to rise to the White House from a minority group and Johnson the second. Kennedy was the first Catholic President and Johnson the first President in a century to come from the South.

Many were disappointed in the Los Angeles Sports Arena when the Democratic delegates nominated Johnson for the Vice-Presidency by acclamation. In fact, the disappointment of these liberals was similar to that of the little boy who finds Christmas Day is over and there are no more presents to unwrap. Democrats and liberals got more out of that convention than any other since 1948 and they got a better promise of implementing their objectives. Those who were disappointed were wrong not to applaud the nomination of Lyndon B. Johnson. His magnanimity in accepting the No. 2 spot gave him added dimension. Had he not, it is probable that John Kennedy would not have carried Texas and more than probable he would not have been elected.

Indeed, in 1960 Johnson was the logical choice. After all, he was a candidate who had garnered four hundred delegates despite the overwhelming power of the Kennedy campaign, the most astute campaign ever waged in American politics.

It is true that Kennedy picked Johnson to help him carry the South. It is true that Johnson campaigned for Kennedy and his own Vice-Presidential election because he hoped to be the nominee in 1968. He succeeded to the Presidency because Kennedy was the victim of the second most shocking assassination in American history. For all that, there is a justice in Johnson's holding office. He might not have won the nomination in 1968 but he certainly would have won it in 1960 had there been no J.F.K.

Johnson is a pragmatist, one of the last left. He is no master of ideals nor of ideas, but there is a real possibility we need the pragmatist. One morning, when he was the Democratic majority leader in the Senate, he listened to four Senators explain their views. He is a man inclined to let each matter stand on its own merits rather than fit each argument into a moral and logical scheme. The night before, the Republican President Eisenhower had delivered a blistering attack on Israel. But in the morning the Democratic majority leader liked what he heard from his four colleagues. He therefore sent a letter to President Eisenhower in which he explained the United States Senate had no inclination to take any further punitive action against Israel. And so President Eisenhower did not go beyond his television speech the night before.

When I say Lyndon B. Johnson was a great Kennedy achievement, I mean the man is going to make a strong, perhaps a great President. That he is a man of intense political courage was already evident in 1954 when he refused to sign the Southern Manifesto, a round-robin protest declaiming the Supreme Court's decision that separate but equal schools were unconstitutional.

Considering the number of our Presidents who have been assassinated in the last one hundred years, we Americans have had more than unusual luck in their successors. Andrew Johnson was no Lincoln but he was no Thaddeus Stevens, either. Theodore Roosevelt and Harry Truman claim history's attention. Only Calvin Coolidge was mediocre. But he certainly was a better bet than the man he succeeded. Warren Harding had let his buddies steal red-hot stoves.

Let us pray God that no other Vice-President has to assume the office because of assassination. But we ought to thank God for giving us some of the men who had to move into the Presidency because their predecessors were murdered.

Campaign against poverty

I DO not know who architectured the Roosevelt Hotel in New York City nor who did the interior decoration of its ballrooms and restaurants. Certainly the Terrace Room is particularly impressive. Heavy red velvet draperies seal its windows. A twenty-foot-high ceiling, a large chandelier descending from its exact middle, lend the room an aristocratic quality. A parquet floor makes it comfortable. Large French doors with exquisite glasswork must have made the entry of thousands important.

I suspect whoever designed it little knew that one day a convention of one hundred citizens would meet here to discuss the ways and means of ridding America of poverty. Whoever designed the room never had such a convention in mind.

No doubt the walls of the Terrace Room have overheard discussions about the poor. The poor have always been rewarded for their plight with a ton of coal, with soup lines, and with a Christmas basket. Few people have objected to the fact that the poor existed. Indeed the poor have in the past proved themselves absolute necessities. They form the pool of the unemployed, an electoral district which can be purchased, a group which can be uniformly exploited, a segment which can be depended upon to occupy substandard homes, receive substandard wages and do the dirty work of the century.

But on July 30, 1964, about one hundred men and women led by Walter Reuther of the United Automobile Workers met in the Terrace Room with every intention of abolishing poverty, ridding the country of the poor in the same way other men once abolished slavery and rid the country of the notion that men can be chattels.

The Convention calls itself the Campaign Against Poverty. The Campaign is in its initial stages. Hopeful, it will be nationwide with an Advisory Council, a campaign whose members will be representatives of social-action agencies. For a start the Campaign will concentrate on education, legislation, and training programs.

Who were the folks sitting at the Terrace Room tables, each of them giving his or her views about the problem? For the most part they were labor union leaders, Irish priests, Ne-

groes, Jews, and descendants of the early Anglo-Saxon aristocracy. No one came from our "newly arrived," the fellows in
the airspace industries, the men with the oil-depletion allowances, and no one came from the American Medical Association, or from the National Association of Manufacturers,
though they had all been invited, even if they wanted to come
as spies. But then one wonders who besides labor leaders,
Catholic priests, Jews and old-line Protestant aristocrats goes
to such meetings anyway.

The Campaign Against Poverty may not win abolition and
if it eventually wins it may not be for a long time. But poverty
will eventually disappear from America because the program
to make it disappear is already apparent. That program will
make poverty a moral issue instead of an economic issue and
the moral argument is always the most persuasive. Witness
the passage of the Civil Rights Act of 1964 which passed both
the House and the Senate because the American constituency
insisted it was not a political but a moral issue.

The Campaign Against Poverty has hard days ahead of it.
It will have interorganizational squabbling; it will have,
shamefully enough, dedicated opposition; it will face, even
more sadly, the apathy and uninvolvement of the poor themselves. But *right action and right thought* are supreme allies.

The case of John Henry Faulk

THE case John Henry Faulk won against the blacklisters is as important a milestone in the path of American civil
liberties as the case of John Peter Zenger. Zenger ran a newspaper in New York, the *Weekly Journal*, which attacked the
policies of Governor William Crosby in 1733. He was arrested

and tried for libel. The lawyer Andrew Hamilton undertook his defense and for the first time established the American tradition of freedom of speech. Zenger was acquitted.

John Henry Faulk was a radio performer who suddenly found his programs canceled, his friends unable to offer him interim work, the networks turning a deaf ear to his pleas, employers elsewhere suddenly cooling to his applications. John Henry Faulk had been blacklisted by the journal AWARE, in the anti-Communist business.

Probably he was blacklisted because he had won an important union election. But once he had been labeled a pro-Communist sympathizer his career suffered an immediate dying fall. There were friends who refused to visit him, friends who urged him to get into another profession, and some friends, like Edward R. Murrow, who stood by him.

There are several reasons why the vigilantes were successful with their blacklisting. One of the reasons is that television is populated by presidents, executive vice-presidents, and plain vice-presidents who never know what is going on. Not only have they never heard of the blacklist, they didn't even know the quiz shows were handing over the answers to the contestants.

When sponsors, working in concert with AWARE, asked them why they kept John Henry Faulk on the payroll, they answered, "Oh, yes, his ratings have fallen," and fired him.

Garry Moore testified that John Henry Faulk could have earned two hundred thousand dollars a year on television had he been permitted to continue in his profession.

Here was a man with no money, no job, alone and deserted, not knowing why, unable to defend himself for the simple reason he never knew the charges, which in themselves were false.

He was a victim of the hysteria, the choking immobilizing

hysteria first inspired by Senator Joe McCarthy. And the scars remain. In April of 1963 an anonymous letter published in the Open Forum of the Greensboro (North Carolina) *News* revealed that a Protestant minister feared speaking out against the un-Christian practice of racial segregation. He confessed he dared not mention it from his pulpit—from his pulpit, mind you, in this the most Christian country in the world.

Nice folks kept thinking, Maybe all this trouble will go away; and in the meantime, responsible men in government, in the arts, in the schools, and in the churches lost their jobs and were subjected to contempt and hatred.

The madness gripped us all, but we rationalized about it like the television executives. We said we didn't know about it, we didn't know terrible things were happening to innocent men. We knew that the fine actor Canada Lee was shining shoes because he had been blacklisted and we knew or guessed that the actress Mady Christians either killed herself or died of horror at being blacklisted; we just didn't know it was epidemic.

And besides, everyone said, "Where there's smoke, there must be fire." What could we do to help John Henry Faulk and other thousands? Nothing, not if we're hysterical to the point of immobility. How many civilizations, I wonder, have died because the folks shrugged and said there was nothing anyone could do?

But we are a fortunate country. There were a few who did take action. Ed Murrow, who went on the air to expose this madness, prepared for his ordeal like a man making out his last will and testament. He was prepared to lose his job, to lose his sponsors and his friends, but he told me he never thought of himself as a martyr. Murrow said he wasn't going to starve but he knew many others were indeed going hungry.

One of those who did take action was John Henry Faulk. He

sued for libel. No one, least of all the blacklisters, took it seriously. It was years before he could get to court. But he persevered and then the blacklisters got a little anxious and offered to retract their charges. Faulk and his attorney, Louis Nizer, said no and after several more years they won a judgment against the blacklisters in the millions of dollars.

By winning, by persevering, John Henry Faulk gave a degree of security to everyone who works on the stage, television, radio, movies, or who writes editorials.

He has helped rescue America from that hysteria. He helped rescue an America which let Joe McCarthy, Roy Cohn, and David Schine lead it around by the nose. An America which let the fakers who devised *Red Channels* and *AWARE* determine who was and who was not to be hired.

His victory is as great, if not greater, than that won by John Peter Zenger, and his name belongs among those of the great patriots of America.

The Far Right

IN THE Russian-language *Literary Gazette*, published April 4, 1961, in Moscow, the following article appeared:

Lenin said that the most ardent foes of Communism will eventually become frightened and suspicious of anybody that does not agree with them. In this manner these extremely nationalistic capitalists will actually work for the cause of Communism by eliminating some of the largest obstacles on the road toward a world-wide Communist way of life.

Every nation in the West has had its Far Right. The Far Right has often succeeded in whirling the people away from themselves and eliminating the liberals, trade-unionists, and Social-Democrats. For it is these liberals, trade-unionists, and Social Democrats who have thus far provided the only effective obstacle to world domination by the Communists.

The New Dealer-type of social democracy is the one heresy the Communist cannot abide. Wherever the Communists have gone they've killed the trade-unionist and Social-Democrat first.

Communism makes no significant inroads in any country which has instituted an effective program of social legislation. While America has been far behind Great Britain and the Scandinavian countries in the implementation of such programs, such programs as we have are still extensive and embracing. Yet the Far Right becomes more and more effective. It becomes effective because it can lay hands on a ready tool— fear.

When I speak of the Far Right I do not mean only the Reverend Billy Hargis and the members of the John Birch Society —I mean also Senators like Strom Thurmond, Democrat; and Barry Goldwater, Republican. Their stock in trade is fear.

We know the United States has an arsenal which could not only level Cuba in a half hour, but remove ten inches of Cuban topsoil for a development in Mud Flats, Arizona, at the same time. Yet we listen when a reporter at a Presidential press conference rises and asks, "Is there any danger of a Cuban gunboat mounting an invasion of the United States?"

There is rampant fear *within* that the budget may not be balanced and rampant fear *without* that the Communists may unbalance it. We worry lest a disc jockey play a recording of Paul Robeson's record, "Shenandoah," and libraries in small underpopulated California and Texas towns ban the books of John Steinbeck and Carl Sandburg.

In 1938, the late Senator Taft threatened that if the national debt rose over five billion dollars, we would all go bust and it would spell America's end.

Well, the national debt is over three hundred billion and things are appreciably better now than they were in 1938. Appreciably. Even Senator Taft would have had to admit that.

Senator Thurmond of South Carolina rises to say if the Federal Government advances financial aid to American education it will destroy private initiative. He says this on the very day the Federal Government is pouring millions into South Carolina for roads, airports, welfare, and farm subsidies.

This civilization, in its worry about balancing the budget, may well prepare itself for the disaster that overcame it when it wanted to return to "normalcy" in the 1920's.

And why? Because the Far Right has convinced people that the national debt is the same as private debt. This is an illusion.

When a business firm cannot meet its bills, it goes into bankruptcy. A business firm or an individual must operate within balanced budgets. But a town or a state or a government does not. Our national debt is involved with securities with balancing diverse maturity dates. When a town needs a school, it issues a bond to buy it. But a family cannot issue a bond to send its children to a prep school.

If the gross national product is high, taxes will be correspondingly high and the intersst on a bond issue will be paid with no cause for anyone's concern.

A national debt is the money the American people owe to themselves. The interest paid is interest the American people pay to themselves. So long as the national debt is *internally* held, the nation is no poorer for paying out interest, no matter how high or how extensive it gets.

Another thing the Far Right says menacingly is that we are placing an intolerable burden upon our children. Well, we are insuring that our children and grandchildren will have to pay taxes just as our grandparents insured *we* would, and they may indeed be high taxes; but these children will also share in the rewards of a greater national product just as the children in a town who finally pay off the bond, share in the school their fathers built.

When I was a boy, this government owed no money. Every year, it announced surpluses. Yet despite these surpluses, there were millions of people scraping together the pennies to buy a cake of ice once a week. I do not speak here of ghetto people; I speak of farmers in the Midwest with extensive acreage, and blacksmiths and grocery clerks and millions of others in the fields, mines, and factories.

In those days any American could rattle off the names of the rich men: Rockefeller, Harriman, J. P. Morgan, and maybe another dozen. Today our national debt is high and no American could count the number of millionaires in Houston, let alone in Charlotte, North Carolina.

So the Far Right is perpetuating a devious scheme. It did the same thing in France when it convinced the people, "Better Hitler than Blum," because Blum meant social legislation and higher taxes. In addition, the Far Right is close to convincing many that Social Security and the TVA and the NLRB are communistic in character and they will destroy our civilization.

The truth is rather that the Communist Party in America has never been a serious threat to the free enterprise system. As a boy who listened to Communist speeches even before the Russian Revolution, I will have to confess the first recognizable Communists I ever met I met here in Charlotte, North Carolina, in the 1940's. It is a fairly simple matter to scare people of the devil because no one has seen him. In America the Communists, even in the 1930's, represented a movement of "chiefs" with no "Indians."

This is not to minimize the danger of spies and subversives. They are here. We have seen them apprehended and convicted and those operating now we will probably see apprehended and convicted. There have been traitors in high government office and there may be men now in high office who have been corrupted. But rarely do we recognize them as Communists.

We fought a great war and came through a trying period. The Nazi spies did not stop us nor did they cripple us. The success we have in catching spies is not attributable to the Far Right which calls everyone a spy, but to responsible police and federal authority.

The most galling defeat we can hand the Communists is to proceed with our progress in social and economic legislation, particularly in civil rights, Federal Aid to Education, and medical insurance, not only here, but inspiring its enactment in Latin America, and let these processes of democratic action become examples for the whole world.

One thing leads to another

I DON'T think many people seriously thought the Administration would follow the earlier recommendation of the Civil Rights Commission and withhold federal monies from Mississippi. As James Reston of *The New York Times* pointed out, Mississippi is the way she is because she is removed and isolated from industrial twentieth-century America. To stop the flow of federal monies, which far exceed the taxes Mississippi collects, would only make the state more isolated and more removed.

But I do think the Commission had a purpose and a larger one than is generally suspected. We are witnessing a reapportionment movement in which state by state must return electoral power to majorities. It was well under way before last spring's Supreme Court decision made one-man–one-vote reorganization mandatory.

Why should Senator Barry Goldwater talk about the cruelties of the income tax when Arizona is one of the states which receives more money from the taxpayers in New York and Connecticut than she gives back? Why should rural Georgians have been allowed to dictate the legislative powers of the Georgia Legislature when Atlanta and the other cities today represent a huge majority?

Little by little the public is coming to realize that taxation is not all Form 1040, that there are matters of grave equity involved. Just as election day is no longer simply a matter of voting rascals out, but of distributing the majority will equitably, too. For many years Democratic New York City has been complaining it does not receive from Republican Albany its fair share of taxes paid the state. The answer to this, of course, is to make each vote count as one and not some as a half and others as two.

One of the reasons the public is beginning this shakedown is because the American Negro by his demand for civil rights has helped uncover the inequities in all states.

My theory has always been that by granting full rights to the Negro we will correct many other injustices of which we have remained in ignorance.

The D.A.R. and the U.N.

AT THE seventy-second Continental Congress, for so the girls of the Daughters of the American Revolution call their conventions, the United Nations came in again for its share of censure.

As one of the Daughters from Montclair put it, "The United States can get along without a world body that saps our strength."

I am quite sure for that matter that the United Nations can probably get along without the D.A.R., but I am beginning to wonder if the D.A.R. can get along without the United Nations. What censures could the Continental Congresses vote if indeed we quit the U.N.?

Of course, the D.A.R. can always get mad at the Peace Corps, the possibility of a nuclear arms ban, general disarmament, and United States participation in the Atlantic community, but then again, those things are no more inflammatory than the D.A.R.'s usual Christmas anger against certain types of greeting cards. A lot of people think Christmas cards are silly so the D.A.R. denunciations become lost in the welter of principles. You see, you have to be for or against all Christmas cards, not just some of them, a psychological fact no Continental Congress has explored.

Being against the U.N. is a matter of principle. The U.N. is probably not going to pull up stakes; so the Daughters will have to tolerate, if not benignly at least legally, the presence on our shores of turbaned emissaries and bejeweled ambassadors. But as long as these diplomats are here, sapping our strength as it were, the D.A.R. can make the newspapers and we will be assured of their existence.

Any Revolutionary fighter with Ethan Allen, Lighthorse Harry Lee, or George Washington by this date must have spawned offspring that far outnumber the delegates to the real Continental Congresses.

I rather suspect the friction between the D.A.R. and the U.N. is because the Daughters are jealous. There is after all a mathematical limit to the number of member nations in the U.N. while there is no limit to the legions of Revolutionary War descendants. In short, the D.A.R. is overcrowded and the U.N. is not.

Were there no U.N., the D.A.R. would have to spend its time in their Congress voting plaques to retired generals who are board chairmen of one corporation or another, and considering the number of generals so employed this could be indeed a tedious task.

Perpetual drowning

THE American liberals have one supreme advantage over the ultraconservatives in the prosecution of the Cold War. That advantage is that the liberals work, pray, and hope for victories over the Communists, while the ultraconservatives have long ago abandoned any hope of gains. Sometimes the ultraconservatives seem positively happy at the news of Soviet diplomatic or scientific advances.

In reading Mr. Buckley's *National Review*, one would never discover that everything hadn't gone precisely as the Communists planned. Buckley and Goldwater have us drowning when our buoyancy is all too obvious. Slowly but surely we have been making advances. We didn't go broke first, it appears that the Communists did. We didn't estrange our allies, the Soviets estranged the Chinese. But even if our victories were debatable, and indeed they are, Buckley and Goldwater are unable ever to hint that occasionally the West has done well. Their whole stock in trade is that we are inevitably engulfed by the tide of World Communism.

Look at it this way. The Communists have met an overwhelming defeat in the Middle East after all their years of effort. Their people were forced to leave the Congo and at this moment they themselves know they haven't a chance on the entire African continent, the most humiliating defeat of all. Even Kaffir tribesmen in darkest Africa know the Communists built that wall in Berlin because they could no longer tolerate the idea of their own people escaping to the West.

Long live de Gaulle

THIS remarkable man, Charles de Gaulle, refused to accept the Armistice with the Nazis. France, he said, was not beaten and he was right. He was right because he was not beaten and as it turned out he, de Gaulle, was France.

He arrived in England with three khaki shirts, a briefcase filled with papers and not a sou to his name. He had been unable to collect the back pay due him as a colonel in the French Army. He sought a meeting with Churchill and asked for broadcasting facilities. The Americans and the British patronized him. He could do no harm, they thought, and maybe some good. But they were wary and selfish about giving him command. Giraud was more amenable, Darlan more easily compromised, LeClerc less troublesome. Little did the British and the French know that, with the exceptions of Churchill and Roosevelt, de Gaulle would eventually tower over all his contemporaries in this most momentous era.

Only a de Gaulle could have brought about the liquidation of the French Empire in Africa without a civil war. Mendès-France, the best brain in the Chamber of Deputies, could never have kept France unified in wake of the revolution engineered by the French generals in Algiers. The blood bath would have been frightful. Even with de Gaulle, tanks rumbled through Paris. Mendès-France could no more have managed such a process than Leon Blum could bring himself to go to the aid of the Spanish Loyalists. They were Jews and thus doubly exposed, captives of the terrible inhibition of "leaning backwards."

De Gaulle did not have to "prove" his patriotism, not even to French generals. He was France. And that was that.

The French playwright Henri Bernstein once wrote that if only fools liken the miracle of de Gaulle to the miracle of Joan of Arc then he (Bernstein) was in their company. With a remarkable insight Bernstein wrote in May, 1943: "If my poor country does not die, the time will come when she will celebrate the fete of Charles de Gaulle."

Jefferson and Cousin Wayland

PATRICK HENRY who became one of the first American reactionaries, accused President Jefferson, from the political stump, of preferring fancy French food, and intimated such tastes made a politician unworthy. Henry inveighed against Jefferson for eating roast beef and savoring the bouquet of a pale pink rosé. "He is a man who has abjured his nation's victuals," accused Henry.

Not so long ago, North Carolina elected Senator Bob Reynolds, the famous isolationist, because he informed the voters of the single issue: namely, that Cam Morrison, the incumbent Senator, ate caviar. "That's fish aigs," said Bob. "Fish aigs at one dollar and fifty cents a bite. Thirty-three-cents-a-dozen North Carolina aigs ain't good enough for ole Cam."

Because his new home had three bathrooms, my friend Wayland Spruille lost an election. Spruille, or "Cousin" Wayland, as he is known throughout the state, comes from the Chowan River area in the eastern part of North Carolina and his home is in Windsor, which more than any town in America resembles Elizabethan England.

Cousin Wayland had served many years in the State Legislature. But what with a good peanut crop and a few visionary investments in real estate he was able to build himself a new home.

All his opponent did was make speeches about Cousin Wayland's three bathrooms: "In the morning Wayland goes into the *blue* bathroom, soaps himself good and has breakfast. Before lunch Cousin Wayland goes into the *green* bathroom, and come suppertime our state senator does not eat until he goes into the *purple* bathroom."

His opponent's peroration was that Cousin Wayland also used perfume, "but you folks can smell me and know I am still one of you good Tar Heel farm folk."

Cousin Wayland Spruille lost his seat, but so important was he that the legislature as one man appointed him sergeant at arms so the old gent could keep a-comin' to Raleigh.

Pappas, Leb, and Wong

THE Old Confederacy was filled with cavaliers—soldiers who went to die for the ideals of honor, courage, and home. Eight of the descendants of these cavaliers sit today in the United States Senate. Time and time again they rose to the challenge of the Civil Rights Bill, deploring the section of the legislation which guaranteed "public accommodations." Time and time again they came to the rescue of Pappas, Leb, and Wong, Confederates all. These cavaliers, of course, were trying to allay worries that Negroes might eat in Southern restaurants, forty-four percent of which are owned by Greeks, eight percent by Chinese, six percent by Jews, fourteen percent by Yankee hotel syndicates, and the rest scattered, as the pollsters say. Not only have the cavaliers undertaken the perpetual defense of Southern womanhood, but they promise, though their hands are already full, the same spirited defense for Pappas, Leb, and Wong. In Dixieland I'll take my stand. . . .

Woes of the political women

I HAVE been keeping you in touch with the activities of the political women of Mecklenburg County (Charlotte). These are the professional ward workers who "get out the vote" on primary and election days.

Just ten years ago, the ladies suffered their first moral defeat. After the first primary, one of the candidates put an ad in the paper thanking the voters and saying that he was one candidate who did NOT use PAID precinct workers. If such heresy ever caught on, it would be terrible. Well, as it happened, this heretic won the second primary, too. This was a terrible blow.

In recent years these political women have been having it tougher and tougher. At a precinct meeting of these "professionals" there were some mighty strong words spoken and I shall only recall the mildest utterance: "Those hussies [League of Women Voters] handing out ballots and election stuff—free."

The worst blow came this year.

The City Council of Charlotte consists of seven men. If fourteen candidates or fewer register, there is no primary, the election deciding which seven will sit on the Council. However, if there are fifteen or more candidates, the primary is held a month earlier.

The political women of Charlotte, of course, like two shots at the money; the pay they receive from individual candidates for distributing circulars, taking people to the polls, talking up a certain candidate. What with a primary *and* an election, they collect a comfortable sum.

This year the women were frantic. An hour or two before the closing time for the registration of candidates there were only fourteen. The women got busy. A couple of them persuaded a service station attendant to get down to City Hall quick and register. The guy didn't have time to change his clothes or wash his hands. But he put up the five bucks necessary to register.

There was all sorts of excitement the next morning. Everybody knew it was a put-up job, but the women sat back happy in the thought they would have a primary to work even though it would cost the city another fifteen thousand dollars. When interviewed, the service station attendant wasn't quite sure what office it was he was running for, but he blundered through. But the city officials and other citizens busied themselves, and the employer of the service station attendant told him, "Get down there and withdraw or lose your job." The guy said okay and confessed he was just doing some gals he knew a favor.

So the women again took up their cosmetic samples and their Girl Scout cookies and their vanilla extract. They worked all April door-to-door and had only the election to earn some political money.

Narrow boundaries of concern

As MY readers know, I have no fear of "population explosions." I believe man's ultimate responsibility is not to prevent the birth of children but to find ways to house, feed, and clothe them. I subscribe to the notion that man will do so.

But this position earns me bushel-loads of mail, most of it portending dire events.

These prophecies inevitably center on when civilization will collapse through overcrowding if we don't institute a universal birth-control policy. An average of all the dates offered for the world's demise is roughly April, 2035.

Every issue has two sides and I would not question the integrity of those who disagree with me. Some of them have even recounted the terrifying experience of standing in front of the Equitable Life Insurance Exhibit at the World's Fair and watching the demographic machine inexorably tote up the increasing population of the United States.

Curiously, however, I notice this is the only tragedy that concerns many of the correspondents. The war on poverty, unemployment, and civil rights somehow do not impinge upon their consciousness. Their appreciation of tragedy often has a wider scope than Congress's inability to pass a bill for medical care for the elderly.

Some of my neighbors, beset by the tragedy of the growing population of the world, were paradoxically beside themselves with joy when the last census proved Charlotte had two hundred and ten thousand citizens and the banks around the nation would write our bonds at less interest than if the city had had only one hundred and eighty thousand.

My correspondents remind me of my insurance man, an extremely likeable fellow. Aside from his efficiency in handling my insurance business, he displays a deep interest in my welfare. He is eager that I become a Christian and be saved.

I have pointed out, however, that I could feel his interest in me was more viable if he could get the same energies mustered to get me into the Charlotte City Club, where Jews are banned.

After all, a fellow willing to share heaven with me through all eternity should not balk at sharing a dining room once a week.

Thus when he tenders me membership I will feel he really wants to have me IN; and when the folks who worry about the population explosion also want housing and medical and employment programs, I will begin to believe they really do have a universal concern for the welfare of man. But not until.

Wanting to be President

Let's take a certain little boy at the age of five. He is one of forty million little boys who may become President, provided he survives measles, mumps, scarlet fever, and the public school system. When this little boy finishes college or law school he is perhaps one of a million other lawyers or graduates who may become President.

When at twenty-seven he gets his first appointment as a member of the State Highway Commission, it flickers across his mind that maybe he might not only become lieutenant governor one day, but go from there to the Governor's chair and from there to the Presidency. This flicker is not an all-consuming flicker—certainly not the kind of flicker you describe to colleagues—but it is an interesting flicker all the same. After all now he is one of a hundred thousand men who can become President.

The flicker occurs much more frequently when indeed our hero becomes lieutenant governor. In fact, even his law partner and his wife and perhaps one astute precinct chairman have the same flicker.

When he goes to Washington as a Congressman, the flicker is as continuous as a technicolor movie. Now he can see the White House, shake hands with its present occupant, get the lay of the land, as it were.

And, of course, when he goes back to his home state as Governor, not only is he talking about that flicker which is a flicker no longer but a Michelangelo or a Da Vinci vision, but the party pros are also perceiving the outlines. After his first term he is one of one hundred and fifty men who can become President and after his second, he is one of twenty.

And what does he say then?

He says he has no political ambitions. He says he would only respond to a genuine draft. He says he didn't enter the Ohio primary, friends entered his name unbeknownst to him. If friends entered his name on a hotel blotter with another woman he'd know about it and probably dissuade them, but he can do nothing with them when they put his name on a ballot or put it before the convention.

Clear and partly cloudy

THERE are only a few men in America who are not considered risks. President Lyndon Johnson named them back before the Republican convention. They were the potential Republican candidates for the Presidential nomination— Mssrs. Rockefeller, Romney, Scranton, Goldwater, Nixon, Lodge, and Stassen. President Johnson cleared them and said he would give them access to all the Top Secret information so that in their campaigning they wouldn't inadvertently tread on grounds where only CIA agents walk.

It got the Republicans a little mad. Barry didn't want to be in the same category with Stassen. If Stassen could look up a secret installation, Barry figured it couldn't be much of an installation.

Mr. Nixon and crisis

MR. NIXON has described how he faced his six crises.

His book still amazes me. He kept running into crisis after crisis and not only overcoming them all but learning from them.

What I call a crisis is if you are a coal miner in West Virginia or a mill worker in Alabama and there is no coal to mine and the two mills in your town have merged and put in automation. And you have been out of work for two years now and your fingers are too hard and thick to go learning a new skill and so you sit on the porch and rock while your wife does piecework at a garment factory. Now that is what I call a *crisis*.

North Carolina politics

Some day I will sit down and write fifty or sixty thousand words about the political campaigns in North Carolina which I have been privileged to observe, from the inside, as speechwriter and reporter. Burke Davis, the novelist, reminds me of the time Congressman Hamilton C. Jones of Charlotte was in the midst of a hot campaign for reelection. Burke was a reporter for the Charlotte *News* and he asked Congressman Jones for an opinion on the rent controls controversy raging at the time. Drawing himself to his full height, Representative Jones roared: "Burke, you should know better than asking me a controversial question like that. Don't you know I'm running?"

PART 4

In Behalf of Ice-Cream Bells

The American way of life

THE American way of life, the phrase goes—particularly among leaders of business, finance, and industry. The phrase is usually spoken in terms of safeguards that should be set up against changes in the American way of life.

Much could be said about the subject. Much could be written, heavy books with charts, statistics, and graphs. The side that fears change would urge that our best course is to come back a way as near as possible to the American way of life. The big problem, depending on who says it, is where to come back to.

The American way of life took its most drastic turn when we discovered the Mesabi Range in Minnesota, which became the steel industry. The Founding Fathers may be forgiven for not having foreseen that the discovery would eventually turn our agricultural American way of life into our industrial and urban American way of life.

There was a time when you could run a railroad any way you wanted to. You could sell transportation to whomever you felt like selling it, and charge what you wanted to charge. You could take the goods of one shipper and tell another shipper, nothing doing. That changed. The Government had to go into the railroad business to the extent of acting as a referee over the industry.

Once you could print your own money. If you had a bank you were free to do your own printing. In 1860 there were so many different kinds of money you had to validate it from state to state. That part of the American way of life changed with the National Bank Act.

Once you could open a store and sell what you pleased, and

you fixed your own price for the merchandise, and you made your own fixtures and set your own wages and hours for your clerks.

That all changed. The Government had to approve your electric wiring before you could open up, and you had to buy a license, and the Government counted your employees and told you there was a minimum wage for them and that you must pay them overtime after a certain number of hours. And the Government told you that in addition to paying your own taxes, you must collect taxes for the Government itself. And now the Government says that you must also serve everybody who comes in, including people whose skin is darker than that of some other customers, and I hear people cry out in anguish about the American way of life. On to the Mesabi Range, they say.

Back to School

It has been remarked that this is the first society to make child rearing a full-time lifelong occupation. It is also the first society not only to be directly influenced but directly guided by schools. Not only has virtually everyone in the urban areas of the country gone to school, but virtually everyone has children who go to school. Everyone supports the school system and a large percentage of people volunteer their services to aid the system, either as PTA members, or as helping mothers, or as car pool directors.

Certainly a good proportion of the central issues in our society revolve around the schools, from Supreme Court decisions to tax-cutting plans.

If the folks didn't buy going-back-to-school clothes, the industry would be millions of dollars cheaper every year. Every one who sits before a Sunday television program, cheering his professional football team, knows that each of these men learned his trade in college. In an age when a small percentage of the country went to school, baseball was the sole national sport. These days when more and more are exposed at least to the rudiments of first-year composition, professional football keeps gaining in popularity.

Teaching has become one of the largest of American professions. School construction must figure largely in what the politicians like to call our gross national product. Nor is there any end in sight. If the giant redwoods were felled tomorrow they wouldn't provide all the lumber we need for classroom desks.

Boys and girls become Republicans, or Democrats, or Independents, or Single Taxers at home, but citizenship, such as it is, is taught in the schools.

With the exception of unskilled labor, most of which is now being automated out of industry, all training is entrusted to the schools. No one gets a job anymore and learns its routine by asking the man beside him how it's done; no one gets a job unless he has had specific training.

When school resumes, hundreds of thousands of teary mothers will put little Cissy on the school bus for the first time and hundreds of thousands of young men and women will be facing classes for the first time.

And the question is: is it all worth it? After all this expense and effort, we are still a nation that by and large has trouble spelling; and millions of us think "finalize" is a reasonable, sensible verb; millions upon millions of us read less than one book a year, while millions more simply read the non-books, the sub-literature about how to pull off party gags, how to get something for nothing from God, or how to make yourself glamorous.

Though school affects every nerve and fiber of our national being, we are still in the experimental stage, still brides and bridegrooms, not yet wives and husbands.

Despite all this, despite even the severe criticism of our systems, the American public school process is one of the noblest principles ever enunciated by a people. No matter where there are marginal people in America—the unemployed and unemployable in West Virginia coal towns, the Negro sharecroppers in the South, the first-generation Americans in our big cities—all of them know the one true route to the center of American life is through the schools. The school system may be a shaky and unbalanced arch, but it is still a gateway wide enough for most, and perhaps one day it will be wide enough for all.

The ice-cream vendors

THE deplorable fact about our prosperous middle-class existence is that all the noble causes are small causes.

We are concerned, of course, with the big issues: de Gaulle, nuclear testing, civil rights, Viet Nam, but we remain adamant in our belief that an accident of some sort will determine the course of events for us.

As C. Wright Mills once said, the soldier in the Continental Army knew he did not control his destiny but he was firmly convinced George Washington did; the soldier in the American Army of 1964 knows there is no controlling hand on the tiller.

As a result, the causes which truly engage us are causes which should never have arisen.

The City of Los Angeles, of course, is now notorious for its persecution of three elderly people who were intent on saving the ducks in the public parks.

Such irrationality is epidemic and the City of Charlotte (my hometown), learning how ruthless Los Angeles was, figured it could be ruthless, too. It issued a cease-and-desist order to the motorized ice-cream vendors who were, it is alleged, disturbing the peace and tranquillity of the Southland's Queen City with their jingling bells.

Here was a cause. Promptly, I wrote a letter to the editor in which I said:

> The Greek scholars in our Police Department have filed their complaint against the ice-cream vendors on a wrong interpretation of a philosophical principle.
>
> When Pythagoras set up his theory of the harmony of the spheres he did not know of the transistor radio and Be-bop or Rock-'n'-Roll or the frightening screech of an empty ambulance or the shattering whine of an overloaded jet or the searing, choking blasts of a million exhaust pipes mixing their poison gas with the fallout of strontium 90.
>
> But man always takes after the weakest segment of the society in which he lives. Unable to cope with the horrible noises that beset us, our police have filed a complaint against the only decent sound on our streets today—the joyous, wise, and happy bells of the ice-cream vendor.

So much for me as a champion.

Well, the segregationists who read me with, shall I say, res-

ervations, jumped into the breech. If Golden is for ice-cream
bells, they are agin'. They said, "Golden's a rich man and he
lives where he don't hear them terrible ice-cream bells. Golden
is agin' all the established traditions of the South. Why, it says
in the Bible there shouldn't be no ice-cream bells."

Perhaps, however, we who sally forth to save the ducks or
preserve the ice-cream bells may some day succeed in creating a
more contented universe.

On Medicare

TWENTY-EIGHT years ago we had about eighty-five medical schools in the United States. Today we still have about
eighty-five medical schools. Each graduating class on the average consists of one hundred students. Thus eight thousand five
hundred medical doctors are graduated each year in all the fifty
states. But, as many die and retire. In the meantime our population grows by leaps and bounds. Thus, the shortage of physicians (created, it has been charged, by physicians themselves) is getting worse and worse as time goes by. Following
the law of supply and demand, medical science is becoming
more and more expensive.

Why not have more medical schools? These schools could
be located in existing federal installations such as the Veterans
Administration hospitals, which are now in the process of
being closed down.

The graduates of these federal medical schools would treat
all citizens sixty years of age and over, who qualify under Social
Security, free of charge, at these VA installations. The physicians would receive a good, fair compensation according to
existing civil service scales. Specialists would be trained and

graduated at VA and other federal installations and receive federal licenses good in every state in the Union.

The existing federal institutions are the best in the country: Bethesda and Walter Reed. The specialized training would be tops.

No one has yet seen the grim humor of the Congressman rushing to Walter Reed Hospital with a bellyache and rushing back to the House to vote against "Government participation in medical and hospital care."

Labor unions and the South

SOME time ago a reporter on the Charlotte *News* wrote an article about the number of "victories" the local unions won during the year 1961.

The labor unions won fourteen out of twenty-six elections. The business leaders pounced on the article with the fury of a hurricane. The executive secretary, Central Piedmont Industries, said in effect in a letter to the editor: How dare you publish such trash? The union did not win that many elections, and, continued the executive secretary, "This type of article, it appears to me, does not aid Charlotte in its efforts to attract new business and industry. Employers interested in moving companies to Charlotte would, I believe, think twice before considering our fair city after reading the article in question."

Now we have it. Industry does not come South because of the climate, the raw materials, and the greater patriotism, but because labor is cheaper and there is less chance down here of its being organized in labor unions.

Anyone who believes that there are inducements other than cheaper labor and no unions is naïve to the extreme.

How much does North Carolina lose because less than 15 percent of its industrial workers are organized? The loss to North Carolina runs into nearly seven hundred and fifty million payroll dollars per year. An industrial worker in North Carolina gets sixty cents to one dollar an hour less than the fellow who does the same job in the same-length work week in Pennsylvania, New Jersey, New York, and Massachusetts.

What kind of a patriot is he who would do everything he possibly can to sell the labor of his knitters at a cheaper rate than that received in other parts of the country?

I believe this entire program of bringing industry to the South needs to be examined carefully.

Where is the gain? You take a plant out of Scranton and hire the one hundred and fifty people in Charlotte. All you've done is thrown one hundred and fifty people out of work in Scranton and hired the one hundred and fifty people in Charlotte. Will you call this *total* growth?

And every operation to bring industry down here negates the whole idea of free enterprise. I remember free enterprise on the Lower East Side of New York. You bought a gross of handkerchiefs for seven dollars and sold them for ten cents apiece. It was hard work. You used your own capital and there were no inducements.

The conservative Southerner thinks of himself as the champion of free enterprise. Yet in order to attract new industry he offers all sorts of non-free enterprise inducements—free rent, free electric wiring, no taxes for five years, a community parking lot built for the factory, and many others. I know of at least two factories in North Carolina that came down here without a dollar of their own investment. Everything was furnished them by the free enterprise boys.

Immigration and the United States

IN 1954, Congressman Francis E. Walter, Democrat of Pennsylvania, came to Charlotte, North Carolina, with the House Un-American Activities Committee. Congressman Walter and his chief counsel interrogated five alleged Communists of North Carolina. Each of these alleged Communists took the Fifth Amendment.

One of the questions was, "Did you write or distribute this pamphlet against the McCarran-Walter Immigration Act?"

During a luncheon recess, I went up to Congressman Walter and showed him an article I had written against the McCarran-Walter Immigration Act. I wanted to know whether this opposition made a man subversive or un-American.

Congressman Walter did not read my article. Apparently he had been asked this question many times, because his reply was quick: "No, I do not believe opposition to the Act is necessarily un-American, but in these cases," and he pointed to the witness chair, "we are merely trying to establish a pattern of un-Americanism."

I could have made my question more impressive by citing the list of the clergymen, educators, scholars, and politicians who had opposed the McCarran-Walter Immigration Act, included among whom was, of course, the President of the United States, Mr. Truman, who wrote a scathing veto message.

I have no intention of discussing the late Congressman Walter in unfair terms. I do him no injustice, however, discussing his intense determination to regulate and restrict the immigration to America of certain ethnic and racial groups.

The McCarran-Walter Immigration Act, still on the books,

admits 154,647 immigrants a year, under quotas based on the 1920 ratio of foreign-born in the nation's population. President Truman declared it discriminatory and inadequate for national needs, saying some deportation provisions were so vague as to allow "thought control."

When President Eisenhower urged revision of the restrictive measures of the Act, Congressman Walter successfully guarded provisions allowing almost free access to the United States of immigrants from the Nordic and Anglo-Saxon countries and restricting the number from the Mediterranean, Middle Eastern, Balkan, eastern European, and Asian countries.

Thus the McCarran-Walter Immigration Act permits those to come who are likely not to want to, and restricts those who *do* want to.

The restrictive features of the McCarran-Walter Act strike me as paradoxical in a civilization professing Christianity. While we have no State Church, one can say, nevertheless, that Christianity is an important factor in the life of most Americans.

Now Christianity became a universal religion precisely because of immigration; the Church recognized the value of the foreigner.

Pope Hildebrand believed the Gospel would be spread most effectively by missionaries *as dissimilar to the people to whom they preach as possible.* It was this Pope's deep understanding of the foreigner's vitality which led to establishing celibacy among the clergy around 1070. The clergy were thus made "strangers" in their surroundings and in its way the prohibition against marriage helped the Church seal its tremendous political success.

More to the point is that we can relate the success of Christianity as a universal religion to the success of the United States in its present position as a leader of the free world.

Christianity came at a time when travelers could go from Babylon to York without a passport. Think how this helped to spread an idea.

In the second and third centuries, the highways of Europe and Britain were filled with monks in black robes bearing crosses. By the time of St. Augustine, the missionary work had been accomplished through this freedom of movement and Augustine was able to solidify Christianity by "marrying" it to the arts. Had there been no free movement, however, it is reasonable to believe the people of the northern forests of Europe might have held on to the god Wotan for many more centuries, and Anglo-Saxons might have taken Mithra to their hearts —the god they borrowed from the Roman legionaries.

Christianity was quick to grasp the significance of the classical stranger in world history. Jesus was born in Bethlehem, a little town the great Greeks and the equally great Romans had never heard of. And a mere handful of "strangers," Jews from Judea (St. Paul among them), were able to "conquer" the great Roman Empire with all its vast works and all its far-reaching institutions. And they did it with an idea.

In the United States as late as 1900, fewer than one-third of our people traced their ancestry further than a native-born grandfather. Essentially we were all foreigners. Indeed, based on European standards, all Americans even today, in 1964, are foreigners, except the American Indian. What the freedom of movement in the first two centuries did for Christianity, the free access to the United States from its earliest beginnings to 1920 did for America—it made us.

The immigrants, particularly the immigrants after the Civil War, gave America a gulf stream of vitality.

What is the reason? Is the "foreigner" better than the native? Of course not. In fact the foreigner or the stranger does not think himself as good as the native and it is this sense of inferiority, this hope to be *like* the native, that has driven him.

Just as the three great monastic orders in France were founded by a German, a Hungarian, and an Englishman, and Christianity was established in the Anglo-Saxon world by Italians and Spaniards, so were the great industrial, intellectual, and scientific institutions in America founded by foreigners from Scandinavia, Germany, Ireland, Britain, Italy, Poland, Russia, Hungary, Roumania, Austria, and all the other lands in the world.

It is a vitality we may have lost since the first law restricting immigration passed over the veto of President Wilson in 1920. When we become comfortable in our environment and there are few challenges, we lose drive.

Another fifty years of "racial" and "ethnic" restrictions and we will all look like Davy Crockett. Not that Davy Crockett was bad-looking, but he didn't look like the Swedish farmer in the Midwest or the Irish laborer laying the railroad ties or the Jewish medical student or the Polish ironworker or the Chinese merchant in San Francisco or the Italian restaurateur in Connecticut or for that matter, the Mohawk Indian who works in high steel.

Realistically, the open-door policy is out of the question. But there are reasonable and providential revisions possible. And they are American. I refer to the proposals made by Senator Philip A. Hart of Michigan. He asks for the total number of admissible immigrants to be one-seventh of one percent of the total population instead of one-sixth of one percent of the white population according to the 1920 census. He would revise the "national origins" quota system by a formula based on the relative population of the countries of the world.

The section of our country which is only now entering the industrial age is the old Confederate South; significantly, this is the one section that had no immigrants, no foreigners, no strangers. There was great comfort in the homogeneous society, yet today when the physicist and scientist appear before the Senate committee to discuss the matters which concern the welfare, security, and survival of the United States, some of them talk with a heavy accent. One or two even need an interpreter.

Lysander, Sparta's great man, was not a Spartan at all, nor was William who started Britain on her road to glory a Briton, nor was Disraeli who made Victoria Empress of India an Englishman. A man is no prophet in his own country. Every land in this world sends its preachers to its neighbor, and receives preachers in return. The millions of immigrants who came to America were "preachers" with a gospel, seeking what the Greeks called "the good life."

It is the immigrant, who, finding freedom and opportunity in America, tells us what it is.

Once we had a peace corps that cost us nothing. It was composed of foreigners who wrote "home" about America and linked us to every country, city, town, hamlet, and farmhouse in the world. Who else better extolled the American way of life, who praised liberty and proved the pursuit of happiness better than the "foreigner" who described to his family in the old country, his new job in Detroit or his butcher shop in Milwaukee?

The McCarran-Walter Act robbed us of this. America's vitality comes now from the Negro, who, striving to be like others, makes others define what it is they are, what it is they ought to be. Perhaps that is America's good fortune, to have always the marginal man struggling to get "in," struggling to prove himself, struggling to enter the open society and "become" an American as quickly as possible.

Ticker tape on Broadway

ONE of the fixtures of our American culture and now a fixture of our American foreign policy is the famous ticker tape parade up Broadway for visiting dignitaries.

The ticker tape parade began with the parade of the returning World War I doughboys and reached gigantic proportions in the 1920's when cross-channel swimmers and ocean-hopping aviators were so honored. Those who witnessed the demonstration for Charles A. Lindbergh will never forget it. The clerks in every brokerage house dumped the baskets of ticker tape from their windows and the paper swirled through the air enthusiastically.

In recent years this demonstration has been carried out to impress visiting heads of state.

But there is one problem. There is no more ticker tape. Stock quotations appear on electronic boards through automation. Maybe in some of the old aristocratic clubs there's a tape ticking away but I doubt the old gents who read the tape want to soil their streets with it.

In addition to ticker tape, there's the problem of the windows in a modern building. Every office is air-conditioned and the windows have long since been sealed.

So how does the ticker tape get there? Simple. The street cleaners see to it. The members of the Sanitation Department spend the night before the parade cutting up strips of paper and on the day of the parade they go up on the roofs and dump it and these same men go downstairs and clean up the paper and weigh it and the State Department gauges the success of the parade by the tonnage so dumped.

It is all done scientifically. Careful protocol is observed. If, say, the President of Gabon is due to arrive, the managers of the parade immediately run off newsreels of the parade accorded for the President, say, of Mali, and insure the same volume is dumped. The parade would need more tonnage for the Mexican President than the Peruvian.

All ticker tape parades are timed for 12:05. This is because noon is the traditional lunch break on Wall Street and at 11:50 all the streets are roped off so the hungry secretaries and clerks and brokers cannot cross easily. They are more or less confined and therefore look like spectators to the parade. The street cleaners toss out the paper, the band starts up, everyone on Wall Street says, "Who is it?" and another ticker tape parade is under way.

Las Vegas: another moon

IN THIS society people mine copper and coal and iron and it is smelted and converted into something else and sold. Or they manufacture automobiles or housedresses or they sell pots and pans from door to door. But in Las Vegas the people deal with the end product only—money itself.

When the mines gave out in Las Vegas about thirty years ago, this remarkable little desert city found an untapped vein that has guaranteed continuous progress. Las Vegas, the gambling city, attracts to itself visitors from all over the world who stand and wonder.

Perhaps this great American civilization needs a Las Vegas; an outlet for all its avaricious, or I should say, sporting, tendencies. But do not misunderstand me; the sole and only industry of the city is gambling. At all other levels, Las Vegas is as pure if not purer than any other city in America. In Las Vegas no one is interested in anything but money, and anything includes sex.

The gamblers who look at the naked girls onstage are restless, and the girls themselves are in a hurry to get to the keno scoreboards.

There is a paradoxical purity about Las Vegas. No woman leers at you in the post office as they do in a thousand other cities. No one wastes the time it takes to fix a traffic ticket. He pays his fine and hurries back to the one-arm bandits. The biggest sin in Las Vegas is for an employee to cheat the gambling house or for a gambler to try to fix a slot machine with a screwdriver or in some other way.

"Come and get it!" they cry and "it" means money. They take inventory in the vaults below the gambling houses every night, and inventory here in silver and in paper is the absolute of our culture.

There's something for everybody in the way of gambling in Las Vegas. The tourists play the wheel, the dice games, and the slot machines. The housewives and elderly retired people play keno or bingo. I chatted with one old gent, now retired, who has a regular routine. After breakfast he goes to the Temple, says his prayers and along about 10 A.M., he takes his place before the board with keno card in hand.

The farm problem

The farm problem is like death and taxes, it is always with us. We had a farm problem when I was a boy on the Lower East Side. We learned about it in school at the same time teachers were touting us to take Spanish because trade with Latin America was the coming thing. History knows massacres, bloodshed, and the farm problem. And only one man has ever solved it.

Joseph solved the farm problem when Pharaoh described his nightly dreams. The Egyptian financiers couldn't solve it, but Joseph, who had been imbued with his father's wisdom, could. Joseph not only turned the corn of Egypt into golden currency but bought up all the valuable real estate for his employer, Pharaoh.

Four hundred years later, Moses, who led the children of Israel out of bondage, reintroduced Joseph's farm policy. He had been thoroughly familiar with the Egyptian program and he had established the policy for the newly freed Jews. They must not ravage the earth, they must build up surplus, they must bank it in storage, and every seventh year they must let the land lie fallow so that the earth may replenish itself.

What the Department of Agriculture needs is a little reading of the Hebraic law of Shmitta. It was all written down by Moses.

Geese vs. men

MEN throughout the world are being displaced by machines. In America there are even areas where men are being displaced by geese. The big cotton planters import swarms of geese which weed better and more cheaply than men with hoes.

Not only the machines which, of course, harvest better and cheaper, but now geese help cause unemployment among the farmhands.

The sharecroppers on a yearly average earn less than one thousand dollars. One in every six farm workers is a Negro and it is no secret that displacement is proportionately greater among them than among whites. But it is bad for the white tenant farmer and sharecropper, too.

Many of the farmers have been going into the cities. To their distress—and ours—they find they lack the skills to compete for industrial jobs. And once in the city they are not able to feed themselves. No matter how bad things were on the farm, there were collard greens and fatback to sustain minimal life.

The Federal Government has initiated some help. For one thing, it has enforced stringent regulations against foreign labor represented by the wetbacks, or as the proprietor calls them, *"Braceros."* It has also insisted on a minimum wage for such labor but this at best simply shifts the pain from one set of shoulders to another.

The Federal Housing Administration has liberalized its criteria for loans and the Department of Labor has instituted a retraining program for displaced workers. Unfortunately, these programs are not equally distributed, most of the aid going to white families.

The National Sharecroppers Fund has stepped up its own program to help make sharecroppers aware of what federal and state aid is available to them.

It is just as bad for the cities as it is for the farms to have an ever-increasing pool of hungry, dissatisfied, desperate men without work. What these men need is legislation. Not legislation to keep out the geese or the machines—for these, I fear, have come to stay—but legislation to provide for their transfer to other industries, and legislation to provide a fair wage for those who stay on the farm cropping shares.

Of the same blood

"OF THE same blood" is, for the Southern cotton-mill owner, a two-edged semantic sword. He has used this phrase since the turn of the twentieth century, and, for him, it represents the most effective four words in the language. The mill worker thinks of the Negro when he hears the boss man say those words, and the boss man thinks of the union organizer.

On the annual July Fourth outing, the boss man emphasizes to his loyal workers, "We are of the same blood." He is making a promise no Negroes will work in his plants and he is levying a tax that no union will disrupt the working day either. The lint-head believes this. He believes signing a card with that "foreigner" from the Textile Workers Union in New York City is a denial of his bloodlines.

When the semiannual watermelon cutting has adjourned, sure enough the millowner will make a short speech about the same blood coursing through everyone's veins.

It has always been an effective allowance when used by Southern millowners or their local superintendents. It is an equally effective allowance when used by plant superintendents who represent absentee owners in New York or Paris, owners who have never seen the South.

Only rarely is this semantic double-think challenged.

Once upon a time, and this is a true story, there was a young mill girl who had an illegitimate child by the millowner's son. The father gave her some money and she went to New York where she worked as a waitress and raised her child.

When the boy was grown and married, the mother went back to the North Carolina mill town and got a job in the same textile plant. By this time, the millowner had died and the son had succeeded to the presidency. The child he had fathered had been graduated from Columbia University and had become a staff member of the Amalgamated Clothing Workers Union. After this apprenticeship, he took a job as an organizer for the Textile Workers Union of America and his first assignment was to organize the mill where his mother worked.

When the mill had its annual outing, the union was still working hard to get signatures. The millowner desperately sought to impede their progress and, at this outing, he told his workers, "We are all one big happy family because we are of the same blood."

A middle-aged woman pushed up to the platform and said, "Yes, we are indeed all 'of the same blood.' You are the father of my son who is trying to organize us into the union."

The Southern wife

THE South, which is the last part of America to retain the values of an agrarian culture, finds togetherness hard to accept. While a married couple in California shares a joint personality and a Northern man is indivisible from his family, a Southerner has both a private and a public personality. The Southerner manages this by putting the stamp of "not for community use" on his wife. The Southern wife does not help him sell one hundred new cars to the local taxicab company, she does not represent his interest in community affairs. The Southerner's wife retains the Biblical value of a wife.

A Southern Jew can spend twenty years on the Community Chest Board with an amiable Southern Gentile. They can do business together, laugh together, and make money together.

But when the Jew visits the Gentile home, the wife always spends the time upstairs. To commit the wife would mean total social acceptance.

The one person who sometimes escapes these iron rules, curiously enough, is the Jewish bachelor, or who is otherwise unattached. He gets invited; he doesn't have a wife, thus he will not involve either host or hostess in another social mystique. A poor Jewish bachelor will often cross the thresholds of mansions where a millionaire Jewish industrialist never goes. But bachelors have their problems, too.

Distillers to the rescue

OPERATING the only legal distillery in a state where the sales of "shine" are two and a half times that of tax-paid brands and where "shining" is a way of life can present problems. But the problems have been overcome by the Viking Distillery of Albany, Georgia. If you can't beat the moonshiners join them. So with a federal excise stamp, this distillery is selling Georgia Moon, a ninety-proof corn whiskey, marketed in the old self-sealer fruit jar. The whiskey is guaranteed to be less than thirty days old. The success of this whiskey in undercutting the white lightnin' is amazing. A lot of moonshiners will have to start drawing their Social Security.

Only in California

MRS. HAROLD DRESSER of Los Angeles writes to tell me of the morning she heard the tin whistle of the bakery truck making its suburban rounds. The deliveries were made by a Mexican-American driver who counted change only in Spanish and often had trouble managing the English language.

This morning he slowed in front of the Dresser house and Mrs. Dresser called to him, "One egg bread, please."

He simply looked at her.

"One egg bread, please," said Mrs. Dresser loudly, going on the assumption that if she made her request more noisily he would understand more easily.

"One what?" asked the driver.

"Egg bread!" screamed Mrs. Dresser.

"Oh," said the Mexican. "You mean a *challe*."

The sad season

THE sad time of the year, I've noticed, comes for some men the day the professional football season ends with the televising of the last All-Star Bowl. It is a sad time for them because it will be three months before baseball season starts. The television set will collect cobwebs and the verve will go out of life and the beer in the icebox will remain capped. They try to amuse themselves by getting elected to the board of trustees of the local Y.M.C.A., or with some mischievous adulteries. There are some who go to the extremes of attending basketball and hockey games, but their fervor isn't real. They suffer grimly through and in the spring you see them walking the streets with little transistor radios perched on their shoulders, happy as clams.

Only in America

THE students of a Jewish parochial school in Cleveland went on an expedition to Detroit, Michigan. Among the highlights of their trip was a tour through the Ford Motor Company.

Just before they left the parking lot to go home, the teacher said it was time for their afternoon prayers—*mincha*. The boys moved to a vacant part of the parking lot and began their prayers.

A Ford Motor Company official noticed this and went to the manager of the lot and told him no motor should turn over and no car should move until the children had finished their devotions.

Brrrummmm!

TEEN-AGERS are definitely spending two hundred dollars extra now to get back the cheap sports car with the gear shift. First they wanted the gear shift off the floor and then out of the car and now they want it back in and on the floor.

I know the reason. The lack of shifting gears does not give the driver the feeling of possession and mastery. The machine goes and we have found that this is not enough. When the machine goes by itself, so to speak, it dehumanizes the individual. They want gears now and they want to be able to shift and with each shift they say *brrrum*, and then the second gear, *brrruuuuum*, and the driver lets his hair fly and he pops the gear shift. Kind of a phallic symbol, it suggests a certain sexual vigor that pressing buttons does not. *Brrruuum, bruuummm.*

Dixie dictionary

You may have seen some of this before, but I thought I'd pick my own favorites—everyday words and how us Sothron boys pronounce them:

Abode— Wooden plank

Balks— Containers

Beckon— Meat from a pig

Coat— Place of justice

Faints— Barricade

Frustrate— Tops. The Best

Lack— To enjoy, as "I lack fried chicken"

Tarred— Weary

Tin sin stow— Ten-cent store

Woes of the middle class

MANY of my subscribers send me authentic *Carolina Israelite* tidbits of human interest from the meetings of the board of trustees, elders, and stewards of their respective churches and temples.

In one fashionable church the controversy dividing the

membership is whether the minister is doing the proper thing by appearing on the golf course in Bermuda shorts.

In one Southern temple the rabbi has shocked many of the worshipers by appearing in the pulpit with a crew-cut hair style. I told an important member of that congregation that the only way out of this dilemma is for them to switch from Reform to Orthodox so the rabbi would have to wear a yarmulke (head covering), but the member of the congregation in question merely said, "I do not think that's humorous at all."

But for a real big hassle I would like to discuss a controversy which concerns the rabbi of a temple not far from the Mississippi River. The big problem in this congregation now is whether it is proper for a rabbi to have pets. The rabbi and his rebbitzen have a great big dog, of which they are very proud; they even enter him in local dog shows. But during the past year the congregation has become increasingly restless about that dog. Whoever heard of a rabbi with a dog? Who does he think he is—Huckleberry Finn?

The trustees have not brought this matter to the rabbi's attention officially, but the talk in the community has become uncomfortable for all concerned. The rabbi and his wife hide the dog when they have congregational visitors, but before the evening is over, one trustee's wife is sure to say, "I'd love to see the wallpaper in that bedroom again," and before the rebbitzen can make a move, the door has been opened and the big dog has charged into the front room, going from guest to guest.

The switcheroo

A JEWISH manufacturer had an argument because one of his Christian employees refused to work on the Jewish Sabbath—Saturday. The Seventh-day Adventist was fired but eventually won unemployment-insurance rights after a bit of litigation.

Up in Detroit, a swank restaurant changed hands and the new management brought in its own waiters. Negroes. The discharged waiters of the old management—all white— charged racial discrimination before the State Fair Employment Practices Commission.

Rigid education

WHEN I was a boy at P. S. 20 you used to go to your home room and after the teacher took attendance, some boys rolled the doors back and bingo! you were at assembly—the whole school was in front of you—and then the monitors rolled the doors back and you had your private classrooms. And in the morning it was a grammar school, and in the evening it was a high school. Like the fellow in the poem, "In the winter, I'm a Buddhist, in the summer I'm a nudist," the schools were pretty flexible.

Now, if the school system adds one more tenth, eleventh, and twelfth grades, it adds correspondingly one more nurse, one more assistant principal, one more guidance counselor, one more administrative assistant, one more driving instructor, and one more psychologist in perpetuity. In the old schools they had just pupils and teachers but those days are gone forever like students who were graduated with the ability to express themselves in English sentences.

Then there's the parking problem. I saw more cars outside of a high school in Oklahoma than are outside Ford's Rouge plant in Michigan. I even know of a serious family situation where both brother and sister who go to the same high school insist on separate autos.

So it goes all through the night all over America. And the high school kids couldn't care less. The colleges still devote the first two years to teaching them what they ought to have known when they entered.

Where are the names of yesteryear?

THERE was a time when everyone had a nickname. People don't have them nowadays. Perhaps it is because we are all too busy to familiarize ourselves with the personal idiosyncrasies of others. Where are the names of yesteryear? Where are Fatso, Stinky, Butch? Where are Mouth, Schnozz, and Lard?

They are now Melvin, Lester, Everett, or Ellsworth. In fact, I was in a supermarket the other day trailing a woman with two kids, one of them a little boy in the cart. As she waited to check out her purchases, the little kid started to fuss and the lady said to the older, "Randolph, shuckle Williston."

Auntie's boon

WHAT a beneficence! If widowed Aunt Essie baby-sits for fifty dollars a month three and a half years for her nephew Sidney, she will get forty dollars per month for life at sixty-two. She will be able to take a taxi, buy vitamins, have her hair set, and feel like a younger woman, and the money will be in circulation before you can say Sholem Aleichem.

Another hunger

CHICAGO, America's Renaissance City, is blessed with a small but active order called "Little Brothers of the Poor." It is a charitable organization devoted to supplying needy people with food. But what makes the Little Brothers of the Poor different from other charitable organizations is that among the staples to the indigent they include a bottle of wine, lobster tails, and mayonnaise. Also, the Little Brothers of the Poor include a bouquet of flowers in each basket.

These are people of wisdom and imagination. The Little Brothers of the Poor know there is a hunger of the mind and spirit as well as of the body.

Harry Golden, Jr.
and the Detroit pharmacists

HARRY GOLDEN, JR., staff writer for the Detroit *Free Press*, wrote a series of articles some months ago titled: "Paregoric: A Legal Killer."

"Hundreds of Detroiters," wrote Harry, "are hooked on 'legal dope' that scars body and soul; dope that can kill—and does." Harry was pointing up the dangers of the opium-laden drug, paregoric, which can be purchased in Detroit without a prescription and which yearly kills at least twenty addicts. As "exempted narcotic" paregoric could be legally sold only upon the signature of the buyer, and sales to any single customer were limited to two ounces every forty-eight hours. But in a single afternoon, Harry Golden, Jr., was able to buy a two months' supply.

And no attention at all was paid to the signature. Druggists handed over the narcotic with no questions asked though Harry was using such aliases as Nathaniel Hawthorne, James Joyce, John Milton, John Donne, Thomas Gray, Jonathan Swift, Robert Browning, Samuel Clemens, and Samuel Gompers.

Some months later, the Michigan State legislature passed an act which requires druggists to obtain a written or telephoned prescription from a doctor before selling paregoric to anyone. Representative John E. Toepp (Republican) of Cadillac County, said apropos of this legislative victory, "The two articles by the *Free Press* staff writer, Harry Golden, Jr., and an editorial were a contributing factor in passing this bill."

The New York World's Fair

THERE were less than a million Indians in what is today the United States of America when Columbus discovered the New World. They possessed the richest land ever known to man. Yet they had neither the wheel nor a language with which they could communicate one tribe to another. Some of them camped by a river and ate the clams and when the clams were exhausted, they moved on to another river. They never had a World's Fair.

This is no silly statement. A fair is probably one of our oldest institutions. The great European cities started when the

merchants trailed the Roman armies and pitched their tents
for a fair. Young girls in the middle ages from Ireland to Cor-
sica came to the fair to find a husband. Some of the oldest folk
songs are concerned with "going to the fair."

A World's Fair is the confluence of the world. It is understanding in its most complex form. People understand one
another best by observing differences, differences in dress, in
food, in products, in music, and in manners. And no World's
Fair can equal a World's Fair in New York. New York City is
already a World's Fair. A gigantic complex of buildings and
exhibits on its edge is a boon, a lagniappe, and a marvel.

The last World's Fair in New York, of course, heralded the
super war. None of us knew what was in store for us on that
opening day in 1939 when we heard President Franklin D.
Roosevelt inaugurate "The World of Tomorrow." There was a
lot that was ill-fated about that 1939 World's Fair. First of all,
it was built to help New York City and every business man
prepared for it. But it was not a financial success for everyone
concerned, except for Billy Rose, whose Aquacade was always
crowded. Billy Rose once told me he built the Aquacade on
the theory that people coming to the Fair with their kids
would want a place to sit. He was right. Another reason the
1939 Fair was not a huge success was because it had competition. San Francisco was having a Centennial Exposition at the
time and "The World of Tomorrow" had to split the folks
with the Fair on the west coast.

The World's Fair of 1939 and 1940 inspired all sorts of con-
tention. No sooner had it opened than some engineer discovered the statue atop the Russian Exhibit was four inches
higher than the American flagpole. There was a week of acri-
monious debate about whether the Communists would lower
their statue or we would raise our flagpole. The only bitterness
I've heard about this new Fair has come from Henry Barnes

who said that after all the work he'd done as New York City's Traffic Commissioner, he deserved a free pass (which indeed he got).

But there was criticism of a more serious nature, principally the charge of "commercialism," which, to be fair, has been raised against all such vast exhibitions in the past. There did seem to be little public enthusiasm for the entertainment projects charging an admission. Some cynics contended that no fair can be a complete success without a belly-dancer like Little Egypt, or a fan-dancer like Sally Rand, but my own view is more conservative. I believe it is extremely difficult, if not impossible, for a World's Fair to compete with the modern wonder of the world, New York City itself. A fair in St. Louis, Dallas, San Francisco, even Chicago, is still a wondrous sight, but there is only one New York, and that includes Paris, London, Rome, Berlin, Tokyo. I've been to all of them, and New York begins where they all leave off.

I was a hotel clerk on Broadway during part of the Fair of 1939. I saw hundreds of out-of-town people rush out to Flushing Meadow to see the Futurama and perhaps the Aquacade, but then rush right back to New York, to the theatres, the stores, the museums, the symphony halls, Radio City, the sights, and a boat trip around Manhattan Island.

And there was yet another widely publicized controversy. It concerned the mural in the Jordanian Pavilion. The Jewish social-action organizations pointed out that political propaganda (against Israel) had no place in a fair dedicated to world peace. There is little doubt that the government of Jordan showed bad faith in using their exhibit for this purpose, but I could not see how the host, Mr. Moses, could reasonably do anything about it. If a guest violates your hospitality, you just have to wait till he leaves, and then think twice before you ever invite him again.

But in all of this let us not take our eyes off this Bob Moses. I never met him but we are contemporaries. I began to follow politics and public affairs at about the time Mr. Moses first appeared on the scene. He was a member of Governor Al Smith's "Kitchen cabinet," which in Roosevelt's time was called by a fancier name, "the brain trust." And I have heard some of his enemies agree that Bob Moses has been one of the most able public officials in New York history. And that fellow has more enemies than he can count. First he made a host of them, upstate, because every politician who couldn't sell his farm for a state park immediately stopped talking to Bob Moses. Then he made a new legion of enemies, downstate, where real-estate values are measured by the square inch and much more was involved when a piece of property was not included in plans for a park, a highway or a bridge.

But whether you like Bob Moses or not, you can be sure of one thing; you have looked upon the face of one of the most irascible, proud, and stubbornly incorruptible public officials of our generation. The State of New York has a great system of parks, highways, and bridges, and future generations will duly honor the visionary work of Bob Moses, who executed the plans and supervised the placing of every brick, so to speak.

And if the 1964–65 New York World's Fair finally does turn out to be more successful all around than the 1939–40 Fair, it will be because Bob Moses provided lots of nice benches for folks to sit down.

PART 5

Scrubbed Floors and Free Enterprise

Scrubbed floors

MY MOTHER always seemed to be scrubbing floors, and every time I opened the door she would warn, "Don't walk. It's wet." The debate about where and on what I was supposed to walk went back and forth and many times I left the top floor by fire escape to avoid soiling her wet floor. No one bothered your descent. It was a common phenomenon.

My mother polished her furniture, scrubbed the floors, washed the windows and everything looked nice. Did she have a battery of implements—a lot of boxes, squish-bottles, and squeeze-cans of cleaning materials? Not at all. She had old Octagon soap, and an old pair of long underwear torn into pieces that served every purpose. A strip was always saved to wrap around a sore throat. There was a lot of mileage in an old pair of long underwear on the Lower East Side of New York.

The suspender peddlers

NEXT to the story of the English who landed at Plymouth Rock and Jamestown, the Jewish exodus from Europe to the United States is the greatest immigrant story ever told.

This story is as romantic as the winning of the West. Yet Jewish scholars have concentrated on describing how a Jewish peddler strayed into Kentucky right after Dan'l Boone blazed the trail and how Haym Saloman lent George Washington money during the Revolutionary War and how Abraham Lincoln had a Jewish chiropodist, because this Anglo-Calvinist civilization grants quicker prestige and acceptance to someone whose ancestors were scalped by Indians and whose brother is a boxer than it does to someone whose ancestors agitated for a minimum hours law and whose brother is active in the settlement house.

Everything has a proper time and a proper place. The immigrant enjoyed the fruits the pioneer bestowed and now the third generation enjoys the fruits the immigrant bestowed. Certainly the immigrant came from unfashionable places— from Roumania, Poland, Lithuania—but I feel it is no overstatement to say the immigrant who squatted under dim lights for fourteen years sewing ladies' garments and went out on strike and came back to a workbench and a shorter work week underwent the same serious hardships and displayed that quality of spirit which makes him one with the pioneer.

The years between 1908 and 1918 were the years when boys and girls wore long stockings which we called bicycle stockings and boys did not put on their first pair of pants, long pants, until they were seventeen or eighteen. I remember worrying so about when I would get my first long pants. I worried and hoped for them because my ambition was to go into a saloon through those swinging doors you did not pass unless attired in long pants. The day came when I shed my "knickers" and straightway made for the brass rail. I was nervous. I stood beside a fellow at the bar and listened carefully to what he ordered. "Birch beer," he said. "Birch beer," I said. Birch beer tasted like Seven-Up. My first drink was a soft drink.

Women's dresses came to the floor. Magazine advertisements were already urging women, however, to wear silk stockings because some of the dresses were short enough to reveal ankles. My sisters had stockings which were silk past the ankle and lisle the rest of the way.

Horses and carriages were the main traffic through the street although we saw occasional motorcars. The Dubrows, the one rich family on the block, owned a car. It was called Winton. I remember standing around this car with the other kids watching it while Mr. Dubrow made his rent collections until we could bear the suspense no more and we prevailed upon his chauffeur to come out and lift up the hood.

The Broadway Theatre was booming. I was one of the few boys on the Lower East Side who knew something about it. Because my brother was a night clerk in a Broadway hotel I was there often, and the greatest thrill in my life was to spend all night Friday in a theatrical hotel on Broadway. The biggest electric sign in the world blinked on and off advertising *Ben-Hur*. This was soon superseded by the Wrigley Chewing Gum sign. No electric sign before or since has equaled it in size or imagination.

Among my contemporaries, *Horatio Alger* was required reading. Louise Fazenda was a movie star then, appearing in films with John Bunny.

Thursday night and Friday morning were the bargain days at the big peddlers' market on Hester Street. Friday was also the day for the Italian peddlers of olive oil, fruits and vegetables, and dandelion wine. There was fraternization in the pushcart stables among the Italian and Jewish peddlers.

Common poverty wove a strong bond of sympathy.

Everything under the sun was sold on pushcarts in those days. Tin cups at two cents apiece, peaches at a penny a quart, hats for a quarter, and eyeglasses for thirty-five cents a pair.

Chickens and geese, hung by the neck, were the great staples of the bargain market. You could buy a half or a quarter of a chicken. Many of those who could not afford a whole one bought these pieces for the Sabbath meal. After a while the sanitation authorities transferred this trade in fowl from the streets to a special market close to the waterfront.

Up and down the street was the man or the woman churning horseradish on a machine. The machine was padlocked to
a lamppost so it wouldn't be stolen.

Old coats cost fifty cents. "As good as new," called the peddler who sold pants for anything he could get. There were
dozens of pants peddlers and they gathered in the middle of
the street, many men surrounding them and fingering the
pants, plucking at the seams. As a prospective customer walked
away, the peddler grabbed him by the sleeve and said, "Will
you give eighty cents? Sixty? Fifty? All right, take them for
thirty and make my Sabbath day unhappy." The fellow then
took them for thirty cents and the Sabbath wasn't that unhappy, either.

There were many suspender peddlers. I use suspenders and I
buy a pair every year or so and I do not think they wear out any
quicker than any leather belt wears out. Yet as I think back,
I'm puzzled at the large number of suspender peddlers. You
met one on every street, his suspenders dangling over his
shoulders and down his back, and in front. There were millions of suspenders all over the Lower East Side of New York.
Why suspenders? Where did they all go? And where are they
now?

For about a year and a half we lived on Broome Street.
Across from us was a saloon and a gambling house owned by
Big Jack Zelig, who was later killed on a streetcar before he
could testify against Police Captain Charles Becker, who was
on trial for the murder of Herman Rosenthal.

In this tenement on Broome Street—the number was 296 if
I'm not mistaken—there lived four families on each floor with
a single toilet. The families included mother, father, maybe
some grandparents, anywhere from three to five children, and
two or three boarders.

But that was only half of it. The other half of the story was that the tenement was a factory; a whirling, churning factory where men, women, and children worked at sewing machines and pressing machines. These were the days before the cloakmakers' union became strong, before the International Ladies' Garment Workers Union gained power.

In one of the rooms four men would sit, one or two women, a couple of young girls, ages anywhere from nine to fourteen, and perhaps an eleven-year-old boy after school, and they were all working on knickerbockers or "knee pants" as everybody called them in the tenements and in the trade.

It was all piecework. The rate was based on the quality of the knee pants. A cheaper grade of knee pants brought a cheaper rate of pay. The average was about seventy-five cents a dozen for the complete operation, which would leave the family of, say five, about fifteen dollars a week. Payment was at the rate of two cents a pair for the presser, and the hot irons were kept on the stove in the heat of the summer (the season), so that the presser (usually the father, a grown son, or one of the boarders) always had an iron available. The children would handle piles of knee pants after the mother and the father got through with the sewing, and pile them up for the finisher. The finisher, a young girl, got ten cents a dozen, and those young girls (and often the wife) were all considered "learners," which enabled the contractor to pay them whatever he felt like, and also enabled everybody to get around whatever laws were on the books. There weren't many laws defining working conditions, but there were some: all of them, however, excluded "learners."

The boarders paid two dollars and fifty cents a week for sleeping accommodations and breakfast, and everybody worked twelve hours a day, the goal being to turn out from fifteen to twenty dozen pairs of knee pants. The ten-year-old would barely earn enough from a week's work to buy one pair of knee pants for himself.

And, of course, all this work was seasonal. Five months of the year the machines were silent, the knee pants workers idle. Often father of the house carried the machine on his shoulder. Many of the men carried their own machines and went from factory to factory asking for a day's work. The average pay of the family often went as high as twenty-five dollars a week, if they worked from six A.M. to eleven P.M. A few blocks farther north, on Stanton Street, were the tenements where the experienced tailors were working, whole families making men's coats at an average of twenty-seven cents a coat. Each was delivered to the contractor with all operations complete except for buttons and buttonholes, which the contractor would let out elsewhere.

Many of these people wept when the industry became unionized about 1912 or 1914. They were afraid they would lose their livelihood. In such ways does poverty feed upon itself. Free enterprise in its purest state existed on the Lower East Side among all the "foreigners" and principally among the Jews, who know all about living in a competitive world.

The East Side immigrant got off the boat, borrowed forty dollars from a relative and went down to the wholesale district. There he bought forty dollars' worth of sheets, pillowcases, and blankets and started walking toward New Jersey. A week later he was able to buy sixty-two dollars' worth of sheets, pillowcases, and blankets and this time he started walking toward Connecticut. At the end of a year's work he had eight hundred and sixty dollars, paid off the relative, and either hired an assistant or opened a store.

The corner grocery fellow who was summoned to the counter when the opening door automatically rang a bell added to his income by selling products prepared in the home such as pickled herring, pickles, and sour tomatoes.

The "for two cents plain" fellows installed lending libraries in their soda stands. These were probably the earliest lending libraries in America. A standard book was *David Copperfield* and another was *Les Miserables*. Several Russian and German novels translated into Yiddish were also staples. You left a fifteen-cent deposit and paid a nickel for two weeks and when you returned the book, the soda water man would thumb through it to see if you had torn out any of the pages or defaced it in any way and then return your fifteen cents.

Tammany Hall demonstrated beneficence to the voters of the Lower East Side, a beneficence expended mostly to augment the vested interest of the political leaders.

The political functionary, working for the district leader, knew everyone who lived in his neighborhood, knew all about the domestic economy and social needs of every family. And the Tammany men demonstrated their interest from year to year.

The reformers and the church people interested in better government were just as eager to help, and for a less selfish reason, but they all lived "uptown," in what we considered fancy homes. They were "there," the Tammany fellow was "here."

It is hard to believe that just fifty years ago there were no agencies for people to go to, people who needed help of one kind or another. The family in need of rent, coal or food; the boy in trouble; the young unmarried mother—none of them had a place to go, even for advice, except to the Tammany clubhouse. At this level the advice and the performance were usually good. Often the Tammany fellow saved a family from disaster; the Tammany organization had a network of co-operating churches, priests, monasteries, Jewish organizations, and rabbis to whom they recommended boys and girls with special problems, and they followed up to make sure situations were corrected or at least bettered.

Second Avenue, fifty years ago, was the main street on the East Side, a miniature "Great White Way." It was the promenade for young people, and every Sunday afternoon it looked like the Easter Parade on Fifth Avenue. Few people could afford carriages, so the main sport was to take a walk. Walking brought a whole industry in its wake—the shoeshine industry. Shoeshine parlors were all over, in addition to hundreds of kids shining shoes as "independents." Here and there you saw a German coffee house that the Germans had left behind when they moved out of the neighborhood generations before, and on a corner here and there you could see an Irishman polishing beer glasses, stubbornly hanging on to his saloon which the Irish had left behind when it was their turn to move away a generation after the Germans.

And now all over the districts were the Jewish tea houses, Jewish fraternal halls, and the synagogues.

But the earlier groups had left behind more than a few coffee houses and saloons. Above all the buildings we Jewish kids could still see the big cross on St. Augustine's Chapel on Second Avenue. And a half-mile up the street, another huge lighted cross on St. Mark's Church, which was Lutheran, and on a street which was now all-Jewish were the Christian burial grounds on Second Street and Second Avenue. If I'm not mistaken, President James Monroe had been buried there, his body later removed to Virginia.

At the dead end of Second Avenue was the famous theatre where the Jewish artists played, later to become a burlesque house; and on the corner of Fourteenth Street was the Labor Temple, organized by the Presbyterian preacher Charles Stelze and where I heard Margaret Sanger and Dr. Will Durant speak. And coming into prominence about this time were halls and "mansions" for the social functions, bar mitzvahs, weddings, and dances. The big apartment houses were already being built to provide accommodations for East Siders who done well, but who wanted to remain in the neighborhood. We kids used to pass these apartment houses and read their names. The apartment houses were not "171 Eldridge Street" as were the apartments in which we lived, but had names like the baronial mansions in Europe—The Imperial was one, and I remember the Victoria Hall and The Trianon, named after the Winter Palace of King Karl and Queen Carmen Sylva of Roumania.

These swell apartments were full of Jewish politicians, bailbondsmen, and lawyers whose business came out of the neighborhood. The folks who made good in the professions, in industry, and in commerce, however, got out. They moved uptown to a better neighborhood, to Washington Heights, or Flatbush in Brooklyn, or to the Bronx. This was the pattern followed by my family, from the East Side to Vyse Avenue in the Bronx, where in 1918 we could still see the goat farms.

Just fifty years ago it took you four hours to go from midtown Manhattan to Queens about where the Kennedy Airport is today. You had to change trolleys three times and you always missed one and had to wait another half-hour.

In the winter the conductor often stopped the trolley to look for wood for the potbellied stove in the car. If you sat next to the stove, you were roasted; a few feet away from the stove, you were freezing.

My one lasting impression was the heroic battle most of us fought against charity of any kind. My mother would no more accept charity than jump out the window. I suspect this fear of becoming a charity case spurred the Jewish people into their tremendous fraternal activities which provided in those days a sort of minor New Deal—insurance, death "benefit," sick "benefit," and unemployment "benefit."

How could "death," "sickness," and "unemployment" be associated with the word "benefit"? This was a good system—a matter of optimism. You did not say, "In the event of your death, your family will be provided with . . ." You bought "benefits" which sounded better and avoided the mention of such words as "death," "sickness," and "unemployment." Thus the Evil Eye was not attracted to its prey. The Evil Eye retreats from the word "benefits" as Dracula runs from a crucifix.

My mother used to explain to me that life was much better in Europe. She told me how she walked barefoot through the meadows in her hometown in Roumania and that the land was beautiful, a far cry from the crowded tenements on Eldridge Street which looked across the street to Waller's horse stables. But she told me she was glad she was in America because here, at least, if we children did not have fresh air and open meadows, we had opportunity. Life was pleasant and healthier and more beautiful in her native village, but she said no Jewish boy, no matter how smart, could go higher than apothecary. The crowded tenement, she said, was worth it. She was very smart though she was illiterate.

These notes are by way of notifying my readers that the two or three critics of my sentimentality do not intimidate me. They say I overromanticize the Lower East Side of New York. Yet with all its trouble, I'd say my youth there was a very happy time.

Bronco Billy

BRONCO BILLY ANDERSON was the first movie star and the first hero to boys on the Lower East Side.

Now he is eighty-one years old and a resident of the Motion Picture Country House and Hospital in Woodland Hills. The Motion Picture Academy of Arts and Sciences gave him an Oscar in 1958 for his contribution to the cinema, but when I saw Bronco Billy for the first time, the movies were called "flickers."

The movies we saw on the Lower East Side in 1911 did not come from a never-never land where the rain never falls or from across the Atlantic on a continent where extras come cheap. They were made nearby, at the Vitagraph Studios in Brooklyn, on Avenue M at Fort Lee, New Jersey, and at still another studio on Twenty-third Street in the city itself. They were a back-door product.

Bronco Billy made his movies in Fort Lee. It was there that Bronco Billy and the pioneer director, Edwin S. Porter, got the idea that if people would sit still for movies fifty or sixty feet long, they might sit still for movies one thousand feet long. They stole the title of a play and made *The Great Train Robbery*. They not only included a train robbery, but the formation of a posse. They filmed a saloon scene and a square dance. And the people sat still.

The movies in those days were a glamorous adventure, for "flickers" had recently moved from untenanted shoe stores and converted vegetable markets into genuine theatres with veneered seats which swung up and down on metal hinges.

Which shows you how old I am because they are reconverting the movie theatres back into vegetable supermarkets.

In fact, it was Bronco Billy Anderson who took movies west and made the first film shot out there—although he used the San Joaquin Valley for location, not Hollywood.

Those were the days of the silent movies. Sound, of course, eventually came, and other improvements too. I remember going to the opening of the opulent Roxy Theatre on the corner of Fiftieth Street and Seventh Avenue (gone now). What made this such a memorable experience was that it was the first time I had ever seen uniformed usherettes, a whole phalanx of them, all equipped with flashlights. Not technicolor, or Cinemascope, or 3-D had made such an impression on me.

East Side immigrant boys didn't troop to see Bronco Billy because they wanted to grow up and become actors or because they needed an escape from home life. We went to see Bronco Billy because he exemplified the attitudes we admired so much in the New World. He was a heroic cowboy. That's what we wanted to be—heroic cowboys. He had the same effect on us then that a stock-car racer has on twelve-year-olds today. He was the ultimate in masculinity and maturity. The early Westerns conferred upon us the first ideals of American manhood: speak truth, shoot straight, and build railroads.

Mouthful of kosher Sapolio

WHEN the great waves of Jewish immigration came, the newcomers knew nothing about baseball, football, or straight pool. For a whole generation their sport was talk. So the principal of Public School 20, Mr. I. Edwin Goldwasser, kept his classrooms down on Rivington Street open until midnight to give immigrants a place to argue. These nighttime music and drama critics, Talmudists, Zionists, Single Taxers, Socialists,

Democrats, Republicans, and Tammany Hallniks, lent the
school an air of intellectual ferment and vitality that carried
over into the classes I attended next day.

Built in the 1880's, P. S. 20 has been closed down. But because it represented something more than a physical plant, a
new P. S. 20, named in honor of the old one and for Anna
Silver, mother of alumnus Charles H. Silver, former head of
the New York Board of Education, opened its double doors a
few blocks east on Essex Street last year.

In this brand-new P. S. 20 is a twenty-foot mosaic, unveiled
at the dedication ceremonies, called the "Wall of Our Fore-
bears." In it stand likenesses of such P. S. 20 alumni as Paul
Muni, George Gershwin, Edward G. Robinson, Senator Jacob
K. Javits, Irving Caesar (the lyricist who wrote "Swanee" and
"Tea for Two") and me.

In those days Jake Javits, like myself, was a lonely fellow, a
bookworm. Robinson was a good student, more talky than
Javits. It was Robinson, not Javits, who was the politician. He
was on the debating team; he organized the theatricals, collect-
ing pennies for shows that cost a dollar or two to put on—a
real Chamber-of-Commerce type.

It was easy to know when lunchtime came. In the classroom
we could hear a hot-chick-pea vendor out in front of the school
yelling "*Haysa, arbus!*" We'd all run out and spend our penny
on chick-peas heated over a galvanized stove shaped like a dresser drawer.

Or we'd go across the street to a candy store we called
"Cheap Haber's" where a penny would get two sticks of lico-
rice, eight squares of butterscotch, or ten marbles.

The teachers used to discipline us with a ruler, a wallop on
the hand. Then when you got home your father would whack
you too.

When a new immigrant boy with no English would arrive in

school we would give him dirty words to answer the teacher's "Good morning." For this, when we got caught, came a mouthwash with soap. One Jewish mother complained about the practice, but only because the soap was made with pig fat. She furnished the teacher with kosher Sapolio for the next time.

Old or new, however, P.S. 20 is more than a repository for the names of successful sons sprung from sacrificing mothers. P.S. 20 represents one of the most visionary experiments in the history of human relationships.

The teachers of P. S. 20 not only taught American history but shared it. The first students in this school were German boys and girls, then came the Irish, followed by the Jews, the Italians, and the Poles. Each group took something away and each group left something there. Certainly the students in this new P. S. 20 this time—mostly Puerto Ricans—will one day write a similar story.

Free enterprise

ANOTHER large supermarket chain in the east has announced a merger. There will be an exchange of stock and where there were once three competitors, there will now be one company. The stores will have different names, but the same trucks will make deliveries to both; the same accounts will process the reports of profit and loss, the same law firm will be on retainer, the same office will do all the buying.

Free enterprise usually takes the worst beating from the free enterprise stalwarts. For example, the fellows who want a high import duty on the goods of foreign competitors. They justify this somehow; "After all we opened up our market."

Free enterprise in its purest state existed on the Lower East Side of New York City among all the "foreigners" and principally among the Jews, who know all about living in a competitive world.

Even the earliest American pioneer got some help from the Government in free land and subsidies, but the East Side immigrant got—nothing from nobody to be ungrammatically brief.

Bat Masterson's last posse

No TELEVISION show claims my attention like the series featuring Bat Masterson. I watch it avidly, often grumbling to myself when I see the neatly attired Masterson switch his silver-knobbed cane from right hand to left. You see, I knew Bat Masterson and he looked a lot different.

I was a Postal Telegraph messenger boy and I met Bat Masterson in the Longacre Building at the crossroads of the world on Broadway and Forty-second Street. The first time I "met" Masterson, he was in the company of Bugs Baer to whom I was delivering a telegram. (How old is this wonderful man, Baer? May he live to 120, like Moses!) As a matter of fact, what impressed me most about Masterson was not that he cleaned up Dodge City and tamed the Western bad men but that he knew Bugs Baer. Nearly a year later, I "met" Masterson again and it had nothing to do with the wild West. Indeed, nothing could have been further from silver-knobbed canes and pearl-handled derringers than the job for which Bat Masterson hired me and nine or ten other Postal Telegraph messengers.

I remember the genial Masterson lecturing us as he introduced us to our foreman. He asked us to be sure to remember the fellow's face because the foreman was going to take us to the Polo Grounds for the World Series game between the Chicago White Sox and the New York Giants on this October day in 1917. Not only were we to see the game, but at the end of the day each of us would receive a dollar. All we had to do was pass out little packages of a new cigarette called Lucky Strike to the fans as the game went on, to pitch the little packages along the aisles to make certain that every man in the stands received at least one sample pack.

Each of us was equipped with a tray and a placard hung around our neck which read IT's TOASTED. The foreman would assign us to sections of the stands, show us where to replenish our stock, and it was he who would collect our gear and pay us after the game was over—the dollar in addition to the hourly rate Postal Telegraph paid.

Whether Masterson was performing this chore for a friend or whether he was involved in the promotion of the new cigarette, I don't know. It wasn't until some time later, in fact, that I learned that Bat Masterson was a newspaperman working for the *Morning Telegraph*.

Eddie Cicotte pitched for Chicago that day. There was a popular rumor that went the rounds among all us boys concerning Cicotte. We heard he had developed a new pitch, that he could doctor the ball so that when it came across the plate it looked not like a sphere but a platter. Every time Cicotte wound up, we stopped tossing our Lucky Strikes and watched. It looked like a platter—somewhat. It didn't look enough like a platter because I remember the Giants won that day. But the Giants are gone from Forty-second Street, and so are the interesting Bat Masterson and the tragic Eddie Cicotte. But me and Lucky Strike are still in there pitching.

When school was out

SHAKESPEARE knew everything and remembered it all.

Is there ever a hubbub as jubilant as Friday's release from school? The boys and girls tumble into the streets and with shouts disperse in all directions. In the lives of all of us there are moments of ecstasy which fortunately happen over and over. We get promoted or win a medal, we hear we have become fathers for the first time, we complete a successful deal, we take a trip to Europe, we begin a moral experience—there is an endless string of wonders we experience.

But it is hard to recapture the joy, the single moment of happiness that Friday 3 P.M. brought, when school ended for the week. Going to school is, of course, a necessary ingredient. The release from discipline created the ecstasy. The boys "hanging around," the phrase we used for dropouts back in 1910, never knew this experience and were the poorer for it.

But perhaps we Jewish boys had a joy greater than our Irish and Italian classmates. Friday afternoon not only began our weekend vacation, but a great religious holiday—the Sabbath. It is hard today to convey to folks in exactly what reverence the Sabbath was held in the Orthodox Jewish homes of fifty years ago. The Irish and Italian boys had Christmas once a year, and once in a while a Feast Day, but we had the same exaltation *every* Friday.

In the most populous neighborhood in the world, a neighborhood rent by the shouts of peddlers and the screams of children, there was every Friday night a wondrous stillness. It was the eloquent silence of belief. The bearded men holding the boys' hands were on their way to synagogue. So quiet was it, two blocks from the synagogue you could hear the muffled chant of the cantor and the mumbled prayers of the congregation. Once the service was over, a boy came home to find his mother dressed in her wedding dress with a white silk scarf over her head. And his father told him all the sufferings throughout the centuries were dedicated for this moment, the celebration of the Sabbath. And we all repeated the prayer:

> Praised art Thou, O Lord our God,
> Ruler of the Universe, Who has
> sustained us and preserved us and
> brought us to this day.

The trunk and rose water

ONCE upon a time, every woman had a trunk. In it she kept everything that was important to her. The wedding dress she hoped to bequeath her granddaughter was there, stiff with starch and wrapped in brown paper to keep it from fading, and the broach Aunt Lena left her was there, and a small, jeweled hand mirror her mother had brought from the old country, and at least one white linen tablecloth. The white tablecloth was the banner by which a woman proclaimed civilization and her membership therein. The white tablecloth was insurance she could always observe amenities. Fragile with age perhaps, the tablecloth could be mended. And it could be taken from the trunk and spread over a table and a clergyman could say a blessing.

The woman always had a hard struggle to throw away pretty boxes and an old fan. The pretty box was something beautiful to hold handkerchiefs, and many a fan held pleasant memories of a long-ago dance.

An attractive bottle could be filled and refilled with rose water and glycerine for the hands, and how many cherished postcards lay in the trunk?

For all our architectural progress, most new homes do not have the space for a trunk. On the Lower East Side my mother and each of my aunts managed this, despite the tenement apartments crowded with husband, children, and boarders, but the split-level of today or the sprawling ranch house cannot. Maybe the house is filled with too many other gadgets: lawn mowers, cars, blenders, and automatic can openers.

The white tablecloth has given way to the plastic one and things plastic do not command love and affection any more than prepackaged mixes demand love and affection. The photograph albums have been replaced by the slides and the movie reel, and rose water and glycerine have a million cosmetic competitors.

The trunk is in the warehouse of the Salvation Army or the local Good Will establishment.

Sitting on the stove

THE teacher would ask, "Why were you absent yesterday?"

And the absentee would answer, "We lost one of the lids for our stove and my mother wanted me to sit on the opening and keep the fire in."

This was funny in 1910. We all laughed. The black coal

stove was a kitchen fixture in the homes of my neighborhood. Since those days, there have been innumerable jokes about keeping coal in the bathtub, but this indeed is where it was stored in many homes, including my own.

Bathtubs were innovations back then. We were accustomed to other facilities. Every neighborhood had a fair share of public baths provided by the neighborhood settlement houses.

There was the public *mikvah*, the ritual baths for the women, and Turkish baths proliferated throughout the whole section. Once a week I went with my father to the Katz's Turkish Baths. A few years ago, in Copenhagen, I went to the hotel's baths and after a few moments in the steam room, I climbed to the top bench. The attendant was deeply concerned and tried to wave me down, worried about the intense heat at that height. But I was used to it from my days in Katz's Baths.

We also used washtubs to take baths at home. The bathtub was a luxury. Instead of keeping coal in the burlap bag in which it arrived in fifty-pound lots, we dumped it into this most convenient container.

Above the black iron stove was a shelf where my mother and countless others kept the can of Vulcan Stove Polish. The black brush had bristles on both sides, one with which to apply the polish and the other for rubbing.

We polished that stove but always kept one of the lids unpolished. This was for toast. We made toast, before any of us had ever heard of the word, with a heavy slice of rye bread on the lid and on top of that a heavy flatiron. We spread *schmalz* (chicken fat) on the toasted bread and rubbed garlic on the crust. It was a dandy meal.

Knishes

THE delicatessen store fellow in Charlotte, Leo, tells me that many of his Presbyterian customers come in and ask for "frozen nishes," a natural mistake. Presbyterians figure the *k* is silent (as in Knox), but that *k* is very important. Please use it. I remember Mr. Schimmel, the inventor of the knish along with its phonetic *k*, standing in front of his store dishing them up.

Mr. Schimmel had a beautiful beard. Everybody on the East Side knew him by his first name, Yonah. Originally these knishes were three cents each and they were a meal in themselves. The knish is really a pastry with a very thick covering and Mr. Schimmel sold them with potato filling or *kasha* (groats). I wish I were younger so I could eat six of them again.

How many remember that fine delicatessen store on the corner of Stanton and Allen streets that had a life-size *tziganor* in front of it, like a cigar store wooden Indian? A *tziganor* is a "gypsy," and this immediately informed you the delicatessen store sold Roumanian delicacies—wonderful cheeses, barrels of sour apples and pickles, and, of course, *misslinas*, which were pickled black olives.

Many of my readers may remember the Broome Street Rathskeller where all the folks went after the show. Down in this cellar, you saw the great ones—David Kessler, Morris Morrison, Boris Tomashefsky, Jacob Adler, and Moses Horowitz, the playwright. Over on Stanton Street was a famous confectionery called the Ben Hur Candy Kitchen and down the block was Mr. Feinstein's Clothing Store where I got my *bar mitzvah* suit.

Christmas at P. S. 20

OURS was a family religion with services of some kind at every meal. And because we needed no surrogate religious symbol outside the home, there were no inhibitions in discussing Christianity and Christmas, and I remember on several occasions we even stood around the piano singing, as my sister Matilda played "Silent Night, Holy Night."

My own most memorable Christmas was in a classroom of P. S. 20 on December 24, 1914.

Most of our schoolteachers were the first Christians with whom we had communication in America and they were entirely different from the Christians our parents spoke about in the ghettos of Europe. Our parents, too, seemed to sense this and it was not too long before they came to regard these teachers as our gateway to the open society of the American civilization.

And so at Christmastime our parents, who could not yet write "thank you" notes in the English language, made an effort to express their appreciation in the only way they knew —a Christmas present for the teacher.

But all of these philosophical insights did not come until many years later, so the memorable Christmas of 1914 was sheer joy, minus sociology. I was in the second half of the sixth grade, or as we called it then more intelligently, 6-B, and my teacher, Miss Tibbits, presented me a little silver medal engraved AMERICAN HISTORY, with my name and the date. There were two other medal awards and then a bag of hard Christmas candy for each member of the class. And now it was her turn, and soon Miss Tibbits' desk was piled high with cups and saucers, individually and in sets, and many bars of soap,

Pear's Soap, wrapped in pink paper. Every boy had something for her. I had two presents for Miss Tibbits that day. The first was a bottle of rose-water-and-glycerine in a little box; and the second, a memento my father told me to give her with his own personal greetings—a white silk sash with large blue letters: SAVE CAPTAIN DREYFUS.

It wasn't until some forty years later that I discovered my teacher's name was *Marjorie* Tibbits. I was not alone in the belief that these wonderful teachers were sexless saints unencumbered by even a usual first name.

It is a remarkable thing. After forty years you learn that Miss Tibbits was a normal girl with the first name of Marjorie, and that Miss Schloss was a normal girl named Linda. And it occurs to you that perhaps they were ordinary folks all along.

But then you know the word "Ordinary" is injudicious. For in truth, they were more than ordinary, they were inspired.

These wonderful men and women in the New York public schools turned an immigrant population into a citizen population—and did it within a single generation!

DeWitt Clinton High School

DEWITT CLINTON HIGH SCHOOL in New York in the old days was the school for those boys who wanted to become "professionals"—lawyers or doctors or architects. A boy said proudly and simply, "I go to DeWitt Clinton." George Sokolsky and Lewis Mumford went there along with some of my closest friends.

I am reminded of DeWitt Clinton by Harold J. Wright,

who was "one of the boys" and is now dean of admissions at the Norfolk College of William and Mary, Norfolk, Virginia. The famous DeWitt Clinton was situated on "Tent Avenoo" and Fifty-ninth Street.

To the west of the school were enormous gas tanks, to the north was San Juan Hill, and to the south was Hell's Kitchen. Most of the boys who went to DeWitt from the Lower East Side walked through Central Park to Eighth Avenue and Fifty-ninth Street. From that point, across Tenth Avenue was a combat area from which schoolboys frequently emerged without their caps and without their lunches. Strangely enough they rarely had to fight for their books. The Irishers did not want the books.

Let it be said, the kids from the East Side were not softies either. There was some spirited action; but in those days it was all with fists—no chains, or switchblade knives or black-jacks.

"I am wounded but not slain. I'll lay me down a while to bleed, and then I'll rise to fight again." This tells the story about the East Siders at DeWitt Clinton.

The Bowery

As a boy I used to walk along the most famous of all Skid Rows—the Bowery. When I sold newspapers I walked the five blocks of the Bowery every 5:30 A.M. to pick up the *Jewish Morning Journal.* In the early morning I used to see the alcoholics still asleep in the doorways and sometimes even across the sidewalk.

I can remember that the only people awake on the Bowery at 5:30 A.M. were the fellows opening up their saloons and cafés. They used to be busy plastering huge signs in their windows, signs which read OATMEAL, 3 CENTS—WITH SUGAR, 5 CENTS—WITH CREAM, 7 CENTS. All over the Bowery were signs, BEDS—15 CENTS. And there were the usual missions with the big sign, BE SAVED.

The clothing stores employed husky fellows who stood outside on the sidewalk and "pulled" you in if you showed the slightest interest in the window display. This "pulling in" was an accepted custom, and a fellow told you he was a "puller in" as casually as someone would say he was a carpenter or plumber. Once you were inside the store, your chances of getting out without buying were very slim. If you took your pants off to try on a "new suit," you were a dead pigeon entirely. Unless you bought, your pants were suddenly "lost."

Whiskey, known as "a stack of reds," cost ten cents; gin, "a stack of whites," was five cents; and beer, with free lunch, was also a nickel. The fake auction store which you still see at seashore resorts, but with a few refinements, had its origin on the Bowery, with one such loud place in the middle of each block. They even sang a song about them:

> I went into an auction store,
> I never saw any thieves before.
> First he sold me a pair of socks,
> Then he said, "How much for the box?"
> Someone said, "Two dollars"; I said, "Three,"
> He emptied the box and gave it to me.
> "I sold you the box, not the socks," said he.
> I'll never go there any more.

"Good-bye Charlie"

"Good-bye Charlie" was one of the earliest American phrases adopted by the immigrants. They said, "*Leben Zul* Columbus" for good news ("Long life to Columbus" for having discovered America) and "Good-bye Charlie" for bad news. If a fellow was faced with the loss of business, job or girl, friends and neighbors would say, "Good-bye Charlie," and how this ever got started I'll never know.

The one-dollar tip

When I was a messenger boy for Postal Telegraph, I delivered telegrams to Mr. Nathan Straus, the great philanthropist, owner of R. H. Macy. Mr. Straus had an office in Aeolean Hall on Forty-second Street. There were no red-tape secretaries and other straw bosses who tossed a telegram boy around as they do today. You saw Mr. Straus himself and he looked up, took the telegram, and pulled out a dollar bill, and that was your tip. Can you imagine getting a one dollar tip when your earnings for the entire week would average nine dollars?

There were only four or five telegrams I remember delivering to Mr. Straus during the course of a year, although maybe some of the other kids got a chance at it, too. Maybe even the manager went over there when he learned of the one-dollar tip.

The only other one-dollar tip I ever received was from Mr. Hedley whom, I suppose, I should have disliked but didn't.

The Socialist press which I was reading at that time called him a "traction magnate."

The beginning of prejudice

THE Irish poor were notoriously prejudiced against the Jewish poor as were also the Polish poor and the Italian poor. The Jewish poor did not exactly love the Irish, Polish, and Italian poor, either.

The Chinese lived only a few blocks away, but I don't recall any active prejudice against them. The Poles, Italians, Irish, and Jews were all so busy with each other, I suppose we all overlooked the Chinese.

Of Negroes there were none, so it wasn't until later that I understood the prejudice directed against them.

We Jews, of course, always presumed that prejudice existed only against us. I can remember the surprise when I first met prejudice that was not directed against Jews.

On the upper East Side was a convent with a school. One spring morning the students, two long straight lines of little girls, came walking out on their way to Central Park. All were primly dressed in blue serge pleated skirts and white middy blouses. They lined up according to size, two-by-two. It was really quite pleasant to watch their discipline as they made their way across town.

A policeman stopped traffic so the line could cross a street, and the three escorting nuns stepped off the curb.

I waited by one of the traffic-island benches watching the girls pass. On the bench were two elderly ladies, one of whom leaned over to the other and said, "They look so nice and well-behaved. Isn't it too bad they are damn Catholics?"

My mother's world

MY MOTHER's world was divided clean down the middle, with no ambiguity or unnecessary detail. She looked upon such designations as "Republicans," "Democrats," "Socialists," etc., not only as "temporary" in the extreme, but somewhat ridiculous, too. You were either a Christian or a Jew and her world began at that clearly defined level. And a bad Christian was an anti-Semite, with no other qualification. If a Christian was *not* an anti-Semite, he was automatically a *good* Christian.

She was not impressed when we talked about Eugene V. Debs and what Mr. Debs will do to J. P. Morgan and John D. Rockefeller. To her, Eugene V. Debs, J. P. Morgan, and John D. Rockefeller were all the same: "They're all Christians, aren't they?" And anyway, the world would never be saved by a Christian. Only a Jew would save the world, but only a Jew who prayed three times a day and observed every ritual and holiday right down to every detail of the ancient faith.

Everything else to her was just so much nonsense.

Sleds on the East Side

PENNIES were hard to come by on the Lower East Side. If a boy wanted something, he had to improvise. The boys invented their own sports equipment. We made a baseball by unravelling a lady's discarded yarn stocking and then winding it into a tight ball which we covered with friction tape. An old

kid glove was a catcher's mitt and a sawed-off broom handle a
bat.

In the winter we made sleds out of hockey sticks. We covered the bottom of the stick with metal strapping and
mounted a soapbox on two of these artifacts. The sleds were as
speedy as any Flexible Flyer.

The manufacture of wagons went on all year. But a boy had
to be lucky enough to find a discarded baby carriage. This gave
him four wheels and two axles which he carefully dismantled
and securely stored until the day his wagon made its masterful
appearance.

The measure of a great toreador is how close he will let the
bull come. His maneuverings keep him unharmed and up-
right. Well, with those soapboxes we were toreadors too. We
used to race with these wagons to see by how little we could
beat the trolley across its tracks. I shiver to think about it
now.

Painless Parker

An EAST SIDE buddy, Sam Goldberg, had a fine experience with Painless Parker.

Along about 1908-1911, a regular sight on the East Side was
a flat-topped wagon drawn by four horses equipped with a
complete dental office. The wagon stopped at convenient corners. After a spiel, the dentist appealed for volunteers who
wanted their teeth extracted without pain.

Sam was a venturesome boy and he volunteered. The dentist
asked him which tooth he wanted pulled. Sam pointed to a
perfectly healthy tooth and said, "That's it." The dentist sat

Sam in a dental chair, injected a liquid in his gum and in another second the tooth was out. Sam laughed because it was just as the dentist said, positively painless. This was Painless Parker, a famous man in those days.

But there was an epilogue to this. Sam went home and told his mother, who gave him the beating of his life.

From charlotte russe to baba au rum

THE delicacy our mothers bought for us was strawberries and cream. We had it at least once a week. The addiction the East Side had to this dish I believe is what has made the strawberry the most glamorous of all fruits. Another sweet we favored was called "macaroni." This is a coconut concoction which is known more properly today as a macaroon. These cookies cost two for a penny and it came as a great surprise to many of us when we left the East Side that "macaroni" was also an Italian noodle.

The old apple shtrudel was tightly rolled and filled with nuts. To be good, the shtrudel had to be at least two weeks old. We never bought it fresh because we knew it did not assume its true flavor until a fortnight had passed.

But the charlotte russe, I think, was the greatest of all delicacies. It was an expensive delicacy—a nickel—but it was a wonderful thing, sold from stands all over the neighborhood from the first day of spring until the summer ended. It consisted of a piece of cake topped off with a heavy portion of whipped cream and a cherry. It was served in a little round paper cup. There was a novelty to this delicacy. You could push up the bottom of the cup until you had licked off all the whipped cream, and then you ate the cake.

Now, instead of the charlotte russe, all the Jewish country clubs feature a monstrosity known as baba au rum.

Where is Gentle Gussie?

GENTLE GUSSIE liked children. Daily, she entertained half a dozen of them in her brothel on Allen Street during the early afternoon when her girls were all upstairs sleeping and there were no customers.

She served the kids ice cream which she made in an old-fashioned freezer. She looked benign as she turned the crank, and everybody in the neighborhood had respect for Gentle Gussie. One day a robber tried to hold her up. With one kick she sent the gun flying, with the second kick she disabled him intimately. While he was writhing in pain she turned his pockets inside out and booted him into the street. While the kids contentedly ate ice cream, Gentle Gussie counted her profits with satisfaction. She found that she had exactly six dollars which she divided among the six children. That dollar was more money than any of those children had ever seen, or would ever see again until they got old enough to work.

PART 6

Concert on Elizabeth Avenue

Concert on Elizabeth Avenue

FRIDAY, November 22, 1963, was a sad evening for all of us.

The Norman Luboff Choir had a scheduled concert in Charlotte. But people have tickets, and artists have an established tour which had been carefully arranged months in advance. I had to pass it up. I sat glued to the television on that tragic day along with millions of fellow-Americans.

The next morning on their way to Greenville, South Carolina, the next city on their itinerary, this wonderful group of singers, all thirty-two of them, and their director, Mr. Luboff, stopped off at my house. They gathered around me as I delivered a speech about the assassinated President, the South, and a few other subjects. And then Mr. Luboff led this majestic choir in a private concert right on my porch at 1312 Elizabeth Avenue in a drizzling rain. It was one of those moments you remember for the rest of your life.

The probation officers

I WAS in New York the day the city feted Gordon Cooper, the astronaut who circled Earth twenty-two times. It was an exciting parade and an exciting moment: here was the man who had utilized the great advances of science to explore the frontier.

That evening I spoke to the officers of the Kings County (Brooklyn) Probation Board, presided over by Chief Probation Officer Joseph A. Shelly.

All America had grasped the function and the import of Gordon Cooper's profession, but only a handful know the duties of a probation officer. In fact, a task of the probation officers is educating the public, for the public needs to know that the probation officer is not a case worker but an officer of the court, instructed to see that its orders are carried out.

It would seem this is simpler to understand than the immense complexities of the space program, but it is not. Dealing with people in trouble is the hardest of all tasks to make comprehensible.

The probation officer is always exploring: he is always checking at someone's home at 10 P.M., seeing if a man has a job, checking with the boss.

It is the toughest work because it is a work which never changes, which only grows and multiplies, the work of dealing with people in trouble.

I do not mean to disparage the accomplishments of science, but it is still easier to plan how we will get to the moon than it is to assess punishment equitably.

There are many inequities, some of which must break the hearts of probation officers who struggle to redeem humanity. It is they who have to contend daily against the simple-minded suggestions for curing juvenile delinquency when they know the whole problem revolves around the evil that cuts off some people from the corporate center of our culture and commits their children to a life on the margins of society. And this is a subject no one wants to talk about.

Yet I think it was refreshing to speak to these probation officers. The backbreaking work of society in terms of the human story is the one thing that can never be done by computers.

Pope Paul VI and Israel

RENAN wrote, *When you write of Jews, write humor.*
The first visit of a Pope of Rome to the Holy Land did produce humor. When the Pope presented President Shazar with
two candelabra, somebody remarked, "Parts of them are
missing." The folks smiled. The candelabra given by the
Pope had but four candle holders while the Menorahs that
Titus took back to Rome after the destruction of the Temple
in A.D. 70 had seven.

The Jews invented, at ferocious speed, a new greeting for
the Pope: "*Gut yontiff*, Pontiff."

It cost the Israelis three hundred thousand dollars for the
visit of Paul VI which lasted ten hours. But the money spent
was well worth it, and the Israelis have demonstrated a deep
seriousness concerning the Pope's visit.

In the wake of the Kennedy assassination, the Israeli security services took far-reaching measures to safeguard the Pope.
Some objections were raised about blocking entire roads, but
these objections evaporated on the day the Pope arrived in
Jordan and was mobbed by Arabs so that only a miracle saved
him. (A fourteen-year-old Jordanian girl was strangled in a
mob that converged on the Pope when he crossed the Via
Dolorosa in the old city of Jerusalem.)

In Israel there was no sign of disorder but no great enthusi-
asm either. The Jewish state received the head of the Catholic
Church with dignity, however. The President and the Prime
Minister went to Meggido to receive him. But Chief Rabbi
Nissin refused. The majority of the citizens agreed with the
Chief Rabbi. The rabbi's refusal was dictated by protocol
rather than disrespect.

Since the Vatican does not recognize Israel and since the
Vatican treats Jerusalem as an international city, no arrange-
ments could be made for the Pope to pay a visit to the Chief
Rabbi's home in Jerusalem. This was contrary to accepted
protocol and courtesy. Therefore, the Chief Rabbi could not
very well go to Meggido to meet the Pope without the chance
of a return courtesy.

Israelis, even those who disagree with the Chief Rabbi on
everything, fully accepted his stand. It reflected to a certain
extent the difference in mentality between the Jews in Israel
and abroad. Israelis were deeply interested in the Pope's visit
but not overwhelmed. The Israelis feel that Judaism is the
father of religion; both Judaism and Christianity were born in
their country.

It was a sunny meeting at Meggido. Israel's blue-white flag
and the Vatican's yellow-white flag were flying side by side in
the wind. An honor guard of the Israeli army stood by when
the Pope arrived. President Shazar shook hands with the Pope
and they made speeches and exchanged presents while
hundreds of journalists watched and took pictures.

Meggido was first conquered by Joshua, who defeated the
Canaanites, and the ruins which surround the meeting of Israel's president and Pope Paul VI have seen many wars over
three thousand years. To Christians, Meggido is Armageddon,
where the last battle against the anti-Christ will be fought. It
was an appropriate place to meet in the cause of peace.

Since the Arabs strenuously objected to the Pope's visiting
Israel, which visit incidentally meant nothing less than *de
facto* recognition of the Jewish state, Pope Paul repeatedly
emphasized that his trip was purely spiritual. But there was
little doubt about it; he implied a friendly gesture toward Israel and the Jews.

Protocol prevailed in his speech at Meggido. Paul addressed himself to Mr. Shazar as "Your Excellency" instead of "Mr. President," and he carefully avoided mentioning the "State of Israel."

When the Pope left for Rome, he sent from his plane a message of thanks to "Mr. Zalman Shazar, President of Israel, Jerusalem." Not only did the Pope mention "Israel" but he addressed the telegram to Jerusalem—a complete reversal of the Vatican's policy of considering Jerusalem an international city only—a fact the press headlined.

A newspaper reporter investigated. The Pope did indeed address the telegram to Mr. Zalman Shazar, President of Israel. But the city in the original message was Tel Aviv and not Jerusalem. A telegraph clerk who received the message guessed the Pope didn't know where the President lived and changed "Tel Aviv" to "Jerusalem." This is how sometimes little people make diplomatic history—nearly.

The Israelis had much to say about the Pope's visit, and some editors took the position that the Pope had chosen Israel to demonstrate against the controversial play *The Deputy*, which accuses the late Pope Pius XII of collaboration through silence with the Nazis in the extermination of European Jewry. Without mentioning the play, Pope Paul VI found it necessary to point out that Pius XII was a man of peace and did his best to save lives in difficult times.

The Israeli tourist office is expecting a banner year in the number of pilgrims to the Holy Land during 1965.

My critics

Ask Leslie Fiedler, Theodore Solataroff, Philip Roth, or Norman Mailer to conduct a seminar or write an article on a subject like "The Jewish Writer in America," and you will read all about T. S. Eliot, Ezra Pound, James Joyce, e. e. cummings (always in small letters), along with detailed analyses of what made Ernest Hemingway and F. Scott Fitzgerald proto-anti-Semites. In reading the transcripts of such proceedings, I am always under the impression that the *Cantos* must have as large and dangerous a circulation as the *Protocols of Zion* because Fiedler *et al* worry about the former more than many other less sophisticated Jews about the latter. Would that all anti-Semites were as obscure as Ezra Pound!

In these proceedings Harry Golden and Leon Uris, like Plato's knowledge and perception, are always lumped together. And do we take our lumps! Fiedler accuses Leon Uris of sentimentalizing the emergence of the State of Israel, and Harry Golden of sentimentalizing the emergence of the Jewish immigrant. (Where, oh, where? asked Solataroff reviewing *Only in America,* are the bedbugs? And why, accused Roth, does Harry Golden paint American life so pleasant as to alleviate the guilt of the Gentiles?)

At the *Second Dialogue in Israel,* held under the auspices of the American Jewish Congress, Leslie Fiedler, addressing the subject "The Jewish Intellectual and Jewish Identity," unburdened himself about the cultural inconveniences of American life. "I move," said he, "through a country where the secular sanctification of Anne Frank has been utterly astonishing and where the glorification of Harry Golden is utterly appalling."

Why does it have to be me who's what's wrong with America? Can I be as appalling as the South California John Birch Society? As the Alabama segregationists? As Barry Goldwater, who didn't vote for the Civil Rights Bill or a test ban? Or for that matter, as the desecration of the American countryside by super highways?

Leslie contributed these same views to *Ramparts*, a Catholic magazine—except in the Catholic essay Anne Frank's deification no longer astonished him since he neglected to mention it. Golden and Uris, however, still loomed large in the Fiedler imagination. Fiedler was mad at Golden for allowing the public to set him up as a minor prophet, and at Uris for allowing publishers to line their pockets by selling his novels for syndicated serialization. Literary wars make strange barracks mates, and all I can say in defense is that the public and publishers move in mysterious circles their wonders to perform.

What appalls me about Leslie Fiedler is that he keeps saying of J. D. Salinger's novel *Catcher in the Rye* that the name Holden Caulfield "cannily conceals the ethnic origin" of the hero—such origin, of course, being Jewish. He's got to be Jewish, says Leslie. He comes from the West Side.

This is literary criticism?

Concluding his remarks to the Jerusalem audience, Leslie quotes Norman Mailer's poem about me:

> if
> Harry Golden
> is the Gentile's
> *Jew*
> can I be-
> come the Golden goy?

From this I take it that Norman Mailer doesn't like me, since the only time I ever met Norman was at the Democratic National Convention in Los Angeles in 1960 when I did him a favor.

Fred Brinkerhoff, a photographer, said, "Harry, you better tell Norman his fly's unzipped," which I hastened to do. Norman zipped his fly but I could see he put me down as one who would assault nonconformity, for not only was Norman's zipper loose but his pants were rolled up to the knees as though he were going to wade across a swamp, although we were only awaiting the arrival of Senator John F. Kennedy that evening.

Well, to hell with it. It's probably harder to rhyme Brinkerhoff than Golden.

As to Fiedler, I have counted four instances in which he centered his criticism of me on the basis of my writings being "popular." I hate to do this to Leslie but I do hope and pray he comes up with a best seller one of these days. I can just hear him crying out in despair, "What did I do that was wrong?"

Beware the Latin American

CENTRAL and South American countries have sharply defined class boundaries. To have money is to wear shoes, buy books, sleep in a bed, have an aching tooth filled, and pay for an operation. To have no money is to wear no shoes, never read, sleep where chance decides—on the post office steps or the floor of a crowded tenement—to have an aching tooth knocked out by an obliging blacksmith, to let people in pain die slowly, and to refuse to ask a sister how she got a new dress for fear of the answer.

This poor man meets many Americans, rich Americans who call gaily, "Bring on your dancing girls." Taxicab drivers always know where the dancing girls are because the girls are really little Rosa and Suzanna, both of whom once dreamed of becoming nurses or stenographers.

The poor are little men, but beware of them. They may be courteous, intelligent, and hard working, but there is a fury in them which a bumbling Uncle Sam so far from the bitter realities of the situation may awaken with his platitudes. The poor man will one day tire of his leaders preying on him, tire of outsiders preaching to him the virtues of free enterprise, tire of the gringos who call, "Bring on your dancing girls."

Charles Laughton in Stratford

THE late Maurice Winnick, theatrical and television producer, agent for many American artists in England, lent me his Bentley (really a self-effacing Rolls Royce) to go to Stratford to see Charles Laughton in *King Lear*. Once I got out of London, driving was simple. Keeping to the left is not much of a problem, certainly not for one who drives slowly. If I go forty miles an hour on a freeway, I feel like Barney Oldfield.

Laughton gave a great performance. Nor am I trying to be kind to his memory. Charles Laughton was the greatest King Lear I'd ever watched and the whole production the best Shakespeare ever staged.

Mr. Laughton was probably one of the most underrated artists of our time. I was going back to my roominghouse to have a sandwich and a bottle of beer. But, lo and behold, a half-hour before the end of the performance a young fellow came along and slipped a note in my hand which said, *Mr. Golden, would you care to chat for a minute or two after the performance? Laughton.*

Would I indeed? Laughton asked me, "What do you think of the show?" just as any actor, and I told him I had seen *Lear* with Louis Calhern, and though Calhern was wonderful, his interpretation was that of many of the traditional critics, that this was Shakespeare's pagan drama.

But Laughton's interpretation was probably closer to the mark. *King Lear* is the one play of Shakespeare all Jews intuitively understand. For centuries, literally centuries, every ghetto in Europe had an amateur theatrical troupe producing *King Lear* or an adaptation of it.

The Jewish drama has been concerned with the family, with good children and bad children, precisely because the good children and the bad children reflected *the father*. The Jewish culture is a patristic culture as indeed was the Elizabethan culture, and that is why *King Lear* has fascinated Jewish actors and playwrights all these years. I told Mr. Laughton his performance reminded me very much of Jacob Adler's in *The Yiddish King Lear*. I continued, "Where Calhern played Lear with rage, you play him with a *kraakhtz* [a sigh of despair], like Adler."

Mr. Laughton got up from his chair, bowed low and said, "I am honored, I am honored." Mr. Laughton got the point.

I mourn him.

Returning the visit of Sheba

AMERICA *is quite unknown in the African jungle.*

In former French colonies, they know about France.

In former English colonies, they know about Britain.

And everywhere they know . . . Israel!

It is one of the most phenomenal success stories in international politics.

Hundreds of Africans are studying in Israel. Not history or political science. Instead, they learn about cooperative villages; welfare works; irrigation projects.

Thousands of Israeli engineers, technicians, doctors, builders, chicken farmers, and irrigation experts are at work in a dozen new African countries.

The match is natural: tiny Israel has an overflow of experts in various fields of development, badly needed by the Africans. The Israelis, used to hard work and difficult condititions, get along better with the natives than any other white men.

Every Israeli technician abroad is conscious of the mission he fulfills: he makes friends for Israel.

Nasser, who succeeded to a certain extent in blackmailing East and West into indifference toward Israel, is discovering too late that the Israelis made their way in his own African backyard.

When pressed hard by the Arab block in the U.N., the Israelis turn to their new friends in Africa who express their gratitude by granting their helpful votes in the U.N. Assembly.

When Mrs. Golda Meir, the Israeli Minister for Foreign Affairs, paid a visit to several African countries last year, she received a warm welcome, as if in repayment of the kindly reception the ancient Israelis gave to Sheba, the African queen.

Excavation in Israel

IN ISRAEL, the national hobby is archaeology. One reason for this is that the Israeli Jews are naturally conscious about history, and the second and perhaps more important reason is that no matter where an amateur digs in Israel he is bound to find something old. A fellow can dig up a piece of

armor from the time of the Crusades or a piece of pottery
from the time of King Solomon and sometimes he digs up the
remains of last week's picnic party.

Former Prime Minister David Ben-Gurion recently visited
the archaeological excavations at Avdat. These excavations
have yielded important scientific and historical knowledge recently and have excited all the Israelis.

The professor in charge of the excavations told Ben-Gurion
that the best digger on the job was a bearded Jew, a recent
immigrant who had only a few years ago left his little shop in
Iraq to live in Israel.

Ben-Gurion improvised a little speech describing to this new
Israeli how he and his fellow workers typified the wonderful
transformation of the Jews from a merchandising folk into a
varied and productive labor force.

As he was speaking, this bearded Iraqi handed Ben-Gurion a
hand-scribbled message which the former Prime Minister read
as he spoke and suddenly Ben-Gurion stopped short. The Iraqi
requested the Prime Minister to help him open a little shop
right next to the excavation.

St. Joseph's Church

HAMBURG, Germany, has perhaps one of the largest
red-light districts in the Western world. Right in the middle of
this district stands the magnificent Roman Catholic Church of
St. Joseph's, surrounded by one hundred and fifty brothels and
twice as many dives.

The story of St. Joseph's goes back to 1529 when it was
decreed that no Roman Catholic church might be built within
the city borders of Hamburg. Along about 1600, Hamburg's

Roman Catholics, which numbered enough for a congregation, asked permission to build a church outside the city limits. This became St. Joseph's.

When Hamburg fell into the hands of the Danes, the Danish King proclaimed the "Great Freedom" for all to worship as they saw fit. To celebrate this proclamation, Hamburg's Catholics called the street on which their church was built "Grosse Freiheit Strasse" (Great Freedom Street).

Today, Grosse Freiheit Strasse is filled with brothels and striptease joints, and photographs of naked women are displayed on the walls of every cafe and most of the tourists understand Grosse Freiheit to mean "great freedom of sex." The tourists are unaware that the street signifies a great event in the age-old struggle for religious freedom.

St. Joseph's stands forlornly in this district which grew up around it much like the church of St. Etienne which shared the street with Madam Tellière's brothel in de Maupassant's novel.

I spoke to the pastor of St. Joseph's parish and he told me most of the communicants are workers in the nearby harbor and factory, half a mile below the brothel district.

There is a Catholic street preacher in this area named Father Leppich, S.J., and he is occasionally joined by Protestant groups like the Salvation Army and others, but their campaigns against the brothels and dives have not been successful.

The pastor of St. Joseph's says his church was there long before the houses of prostitution and will be there when they are gone.

"We appear to be a weak antagonist," he said, "facing a massive assault by the world of flesh and sin surrounding us, but we must live in hope."

My degree at Belmont Abbey

A NUMBER of people have written me, "I see where the Catholics are giving you a degree." They referred to the announcement that the Benedictine college, Belmont Abbey, has awarded me a degree of Doctor of Humane Letters. But the statement about the Catholics giving me a degree parallels the stereotype thinking of many Gentiles that all the Jews meet in some cellar once a week.

I am certain that I would have pondered a bit in wonder about an award from, say, the Jesuits or the Dominicans, or the Knights of Columbus. There are indeed Catholics around the country, certainly William Buckley, Jr., of the *National Review*, who will look with less than enthusiasm upon this honor that has come to me. And when I refer to the Dominicans and Jesuits, I do not want this to be construed as criticism. I merely want to emphasize that there *are* differences, that Catholics are *people* first, like everybody else. The Dominicans and the Jesuits have contended with each other across the years, and there is a bit of folklore concerning this family argument. It is said that it reached such proportions that God Himself intervened and (say the Jesuits) sent a message from heaven, "Stop this silly argument . . . no Catholic order is better than another, each is equal." It was signed, GOD, S.J.

The honor from Belmont Abbey is welcome. To this Jewish writer and reporter it is clear that the Catholic interracial movement and the Benedictines are people who have their eyes on heaven and their feet on the ground.

And besides, the Benedictines are famous for having concocted the most delicious home brew in all the history of mankind.

Uplifting the Russians

ONE wheat sale does not an Iron Curtain penetrate nor a single test ban a peaceful ally make. But there's more than one way to skin the cat. A multiplicity of foils waits in our Cold War arsenal. They come in various shapes and sizes, as you will see.

Secretary of Commerce Luther H. Hodges recently dispatched to the Soviet Union the United States Soft Goods Delegation, a mission of five prominent clothing manufacturers. The only woman among these plenipotentiaries was charming seventy-seven-year-old Ida Rosenthal, chairman of the board of Maidenform, Inc., a lady known popularly as the matriarch of the uplift industry.

The idea behind this exchange program, of course, is the hope that if we can appeal to the vanity of the Russian female we may get the mind of the Russian male off underground testing. The strategy is particularly appropriate at this time.

Thirty years ago, when Mrs. Rosenthal last visited the Soviet Union, Russian fashion consisted of a babushka and a big smock. She reports that while Russian women are no fashion plates today, at least they are beginning to realize their dresses ought to accommodate their figures rather than the other way around.

The Russians need Mrs. Rosenthal a lot more than Maidenform needs business. The big Russian mamma has vanished but there are one hundred million others looking like sulky voluptuaries with not an "A" cup in the bunch. At best the government can supply them with one brassiere a year which takes a week's salary to buy and requires at least one day's wait in a long queue. When you remember that the average American girl can lay in a year's supply during one lunch hour with time and money left over to visit her mutual fund broker, it's understandable why the Russians insist on a news blackout.

Long ago, the Russians gave up the fur hat, the caftan, and the big black boots. Their clothes are not too different from our own, although it is true that Soviet diplomats and statesmen dress like mechanics who have been unemployed for a long time. The more they discover chic, the easier it will be to deal with them.

It's the bearded Cubans, running around in fatigues, their machine guns slung like accessories, who give us headaches.

And the Chinese—well, the less said about their style in both dress and deportment, the better.

Secretary Hodges is to be congratulated on his subtlety in assigning Mrs. Rosenthal to the delegation. She is a lady fired with the idea of making the peoples of the world bosom buddies.

California, Cuba, and the Chinese

CALIFORNIA is a veritable pansy bed of different races and colors. Yet the Californians, as a rule, do not cross racial lines to marry. Governor Pat Brown encouraged the passage of a bill to forbid the question of "race" on marriage licenses, thinking perhaps people would flock to California to get married and avoid the racial restrictions elsewhere. People still come to California all right, but if they marry, they marry within their own tribe and marry people who worship in the same church. A glum Chinese mother is the only exception we have noted. She is distressed because her son is marrying a Japanese girl.

But California is not the only place where the Chinese fare badly.

The Cubans are worried. Fidel Castro wants Chinese Communist technicians to immigrate to Cuba.

Now all of Latin America dreads the Chinese. Latins feel somewhat mistakenly that all the Chinese are interested in is opium and, besides, they are atheists. Religious sensibilities run deep in Latin America. Even if the average Cuban loudly voices his atheism—he doesn't want his sister to marry one.

Eddie Cantor grows younger

READING a book by Eddie Cantor or visiting him at his home in Beverly Hills makes me realize what a distorted idea young people have of age. In 6-B, which would have made me about twelve years old, I had a delightful teacher. Like all children I thought of her as an old lady. Some years later, I met her at a summer resort; we had dinner, took a stroll together, and I overheard someone say, "A fine-looking couple." When I was twelve years old in 6-B, she was probably all of seventeen.

Now Eddie Cantor is seventy-one years old (till one hundred and twenty), and I am sixty-one. Yet when I paid fifteen cents to sit in the balcony of "Loew's Avenue B" and saw Eddie Cantor on the stage, I had no idea that he and I would become contemporaries.

Eddie's latest book, As I Remember Them, is about the

folks he knew in show business during the last fifty years. Eddie writes about Jack Benny, W. C. Fields, George Jessel, Jimmy Durante, Fannie Brice, Al Jolson, Groucho Marx, Greta Garbo, Will Rogers, Judy Garland, Danny Kaye—you know the rest of the names.

Eddie loves them all. He hasn't a harsh word for anyone. I'm sure there were some bastards among the show folks he knew, as there are in any profession. You won't find out from Eddie who they were.

I discussed some of the bastards with him but all I got was a tolerant smile; he wouldn't know how to go for the jugular even if he were disposed to do so.

Eddie pours it out for the other fellow. There were people he introduced to show business, some of the top names in the profession; there was the money he lent Ziegfeld, his boss, when the master of the *Follies* was in trouble; he helped create the March of Dimes idea; he gave help to innumerable people; he lavished affection on his family; he pioneered against racial discrimination in vaudeville, which deserves, at least, a footnote in a definitive work on the subject; he is a thoroughly good man. But he doesn't mention these things.

I was deeply interested in his chapter on W. C. Fields and the photograph of a scene from the 1918 *Follies* showing Fields, Will Rogers, Harry Kelly, Lillian Lorraine, and Eddie Cantor. I knew Lillian Lorraine, the most famous beauty of the *Follies*. I met her when I was a clerk in my brother's Hotel Markwell on West Forty-ninth Street in the early 1930's. She was at the end of her career then.

Miss Lorraine had a serious alcohol problem, and she was seated in the vestry of St. Malachy's Church, the famous Actor's Chapel, telling Father Leonard she needed help. Father Leonard asked her about all her friends and Miss Lorraine made a list of them, from William Randolph Hearst down to

George S. Kaufman. My name was on the list at the very bottom. Father Leonard, wise to the ways of the world, said, "There's only one live one in the whole bunch," and that's how I came to give Miss Lorraine a room for three weeks to help her get on her feet. Fannie Brice took her to a department store and bought clothes and she made an appointment for Miss Lorraine to see some people for a job, perhaps as a receptionist or clerk.

Miss Lorraine had fallen down the steps of the Amsterdam Roof a few years before and she limped. But she was as beautiful as ever. I have never in my life seen a woman even in a complete state of alcoholism still retain her beauty as did Lillian Lorraine.

But it was a hopeless task. At the end of ten days we discovered that Miss Lorraine had exchanged all Fannie Brice's dresses and shoes for gin. It was a terrible sickness and a tragedy. Later I heard that Miss Lorraine and her lawyer had received a settlement from M-G-M. In the picture *The Great Ziegfeld*, they showed a character in the film falling down those steps on the roof of the Amsterdam Theater while drunk. It was undoubtedly the story of Lillian.

I do not know how much money she received or whether she received any. A year later, I was sitting quietly at my desk at the New York *Post* when the boy told me a lady wanted to see me. I went to the waiting room and there was Lillian Lorraine. There was a taxi downstairs with ten dollars on the meter and the driver threatened to take her to the station house. I paid the taxi fellow and gave him an extra dollar to take her to the address she wanted.

It was the last I saw or heard of Lillian Lorraine, the tortured soul with exquisite beauty. Years later in Charlotte, North Carolina, I read about her death.

Enjoying the scenery

I AM no scenery man. I am always talking, always
interested in the conversation, with the result that the River
Rhine looked much like North Carolina's Catawba to me. I
am, however, willing to pay the price. If I don't see all there is
to see, still I get to hear all there is to hear.

The one American scene that stops me talking, however, is
the view from Carl Sandburg's front porch in Flat Rock,
North Carolina. The Sandburg farm is called Connemara. The
house mounts the crest of a wooded hill and from the top of
the front-door steps a man can see the land stretch down,
smooth as silk, to the lake below, and from the lake roll away
for miles in every direction into the Sapphire Hills of the Great
Smoky Mountains. Even on a cloudy day Mount Mitchell is
visible.

The first time I looked upon this breath-taking scene from
the porch of the antebellum mansion I told Carl, "Your old
Socialist colleagues up in Wisconsin must be turning over in
their graves."

A walk in Teheran

WHEN I was in Teheran, I took a long afternoon walk
from my hotel to the ghetto. As I departed from the ghetto it
was growing dark. The folks I had visited never heard of a
telephone and no one had the remotest idea of how to sum-
mon transportation. There was nothing for it except to make

the one-mile hike back to the hotel. It was very dark now and I walked through the most bewildering poverty I had ever seen. Furtive figures glided by and strange sounds rent the night. Yet it never made me nervous. Nothing would happen. I was perfectly safe and I knew it.

Yet in New York City a little twelve-year-old girl was murdered in her apartment. And that's not all. She was murdered while the tenants were promised police cordons and while still other tenants were organizing vigilante committees.

We have yet to solve the mysteries of civilization and the hardships it imposes.

Living to 120 years

WITH an open-door policy that accepted the maimed, the halt, the blind, the ill, and afflicted of every land, Israel has the lowest mortality rate in the world. A baby born in Israel has a better chance of surviving than a child born in the United States, Britain, France, or Germany. Great strides are being taken to solve mental health problems, and Israel is setting new standards in human well-being.

The rabbi writes

FROM a rabbi comes an order for a subscription to *The Carolina Israelite* along with an apology. "I'm sorry to say," writes the rabbi, "that I doubt whether I can solicit subscriptions for you among my congregation. The people of this congregation do not read at all; all they do is talk, talk, talk, and talk nonsense at that."

Don't worry, Rabbi, we'll get along.

PART 7

Boxcar Annie, the Beatles, and Puccini

The Beatles

"It offends me to the soul to hear a robustious peri-wigpated fellow tear a passion to tatters, to very rags, to split the ears of the groundlings, who for the most part are capable of nothing but inexplicable dumb shows and noise. I would have such a fellow whipped."—HAMLET

The most surprising thing about the Beatles is that once singing and stamping and strumming and thumping, these four rock-'n'-rollers from Liverpool, England, have no discernible English accent. They belt "A Love Like This Has Got to Make You Gla-ad," and hearing them one can easily imagine oneself at an amateur night in the school auditorium back in Kanawha County, West Virginia, or Hempstead, Long Island. Theatre friends assure me this observation is correct: the English do not betray an accent when they sing (Rex Harrison didn't sing but talked in *My Fair Lady*).

The diction of the Beatles thus is indistinguishable from that of any untutored, uninstructed American intoning mindless lyrics.

Just as the Beatles democratically slur their syllables, so do they conspire to look alike. All affect the same head and a half of hair, wear the same drainpipe trousers, Cuban-heeled boots, and button-up jackets. When they smile, all of them have the same bad English teeth. One suspects their proper names are almost an afterthought. Onstage they are the Beatles, and if a screaming teen-ager, transported to ecstasy by thoughts of a gladdening love, likes one, she likes them all. I am not sure I disapprove of any custom which spreads the affection around but I will stake my life it is this simultaneous identity which has nourished their immense popularity.

You must remember we Americans are always at pains to welcome more of the same thing.

Now as to their significance as a cultural phenomenon: it's the haircut, of course. The hair makes all of these fellows resemble skinny girls.

On the Lower East Side of New York City, the immigrant Jewish mothers always put their baby boys in dresses and made them wear a Buster Brown hairdo. The impulse of these mothers was not to make the boys into girls, but to ward off the Evil Eye. Immigrant Jews believed the Evil Eye was occupied in claiming sons, not daughters. Mothers tried to thwart this by disguising their children.

I thought this superstition strictly Jewish but in the last few years I've learned it is universal. The wealthy Chinese used to dress male children in tattered clothes so the Evil Eye would think them poor, and a Japanese industrialist told me recently that many a father in Tokyo insists his boys wear their overcoats inside out so the Evil Eye will be fooled.

I doubt, however, the Beatles are trying to escape harm from the Evil Eye by wearing long hair. The Beatles wear long hair and look like girls not to advertise homosexuality but to suggest impotence. Remember, the Beatles have emerged from the Britain of Prime Minister Alex Douglas-Home; one cannot imagine them emerging from the Britain of Winston Churchill.

Just as the Beatles had to come from a certain kind of England, so did they have to come to a certain kind of America. They would never have attracted an audience of Irish immigrants from Hell's Kitchen, or Italian immigrants from Little Italy, or Jewish immigrants from the Lower East Side, or native-born farm boys from Montana or Iowa or Georgia.

Those were generations that had something to do—the immigrants to be Americans and the Americans to make the continent into a playpen. Even today, I notice the Beatles do not have large Negro or Puerto Rican followings.

Neither the Beatles nor youth anywhere can be subtracted, disassociated, or separated from the adult society through which they move. Ralph Waldo Emerson wrote that living is what a man thinks about all day. While I do not for a minute presume we adults think Beatles or nightmare Beatles, still these four young Englishmen represent to their teen-age audiences an insecurity alive in the world today.

We are no longer what Stendhal called "passengers" through life. The young, imitating us, do not look upon life as an adventure but as an exercise in self-analysis. Where we worry about the constant imbalance in a society menaced by wars hot and cold, the hydrogen bomb, upset by the new nations of the world, and political upheavals, the young worry about what is going to happen to them. They borrow the fears, anxieties, and longings of adults.

The young feel that they are anonymous and here come the Beatles, secure because they all look alike; the young feel they are weak and here come the Beatles proud of impotence; the young worry about purpose and getting the grades for college and here come the Beatles with neither form nor sense to their music.

And it works: the Beatles are not only rich, they are loved.

Mommy and Daddy cannot understand the Beatles, but the young are alienated from the family anyway.

Probably the Beatles' success is only transitory. I recall in the late 1930's how shocked we were to learn our sons and daughters were dancing in the aisles of the Paramount Theatre to the swing of Benny Goodman. Then they shrieked whenever Frank Sinatra stepped before a microphone. But two years later these children were storming Guadalcanal and making the daylight bomb runs over Europe and enlisting in the WAC and rolling bandages in the USO.

The world situation today is much more crucial. Life promises to be more grueling and worrisome, and society itself is at stake. Some of these boys and girls mobbing the hotel corridors for a peek at the Beatles may soon be filing applications for service in the Peace Corps. Some, of course, will wind up in Sing Sing. We would be as silly and extreme as youth itself if we said the Beatles were all-corrupting. If youth is corrupted, we corrupted them, not four fops on the *Ed Sullivan Show*.

A last visit with John F. Kennedy

THE Irish say very seriously they are descended from Irish kings. Probably in the old days there was a king every ten miles or so, and everyone gathered under each king's protection was related to him by ties of blood.

The old Irish legends tell of tall men full of grace and dignity, brave, wise, generously giving of themselves for the good of all. These were the kings of Ireland.

They seemed only legends until we were given one of their sons for too brief a time. Now we know the legends are true. We can send down words telling of noble deeds that will become legends in their turn of a great and beloved leader, John Fitzgerald Kennedy, worthy son of kingly forebears.

John F. Kennedy's name will be associated with the struggle for human rights as long as we have language to express it.

The late President realized there was some chance that the civil rights controversy could cost him reelection in 1964, but he told me that despite this risk there was no turning back.

When Robert F. Kennedy took the oath as Attorney General, Senator James Eastland of Mississippi confided to the new Cabinet officer that the Justice Department had never brought a civil rights suit in Mississippi. By the time of John F. Kennedy's assassination, however, the Justice Department had initiated history's largest number of civil rights suits charging discrimination in voting, including the biggest one of all, the United States v. Mississippi.

President Kennedy met the challenge the segregationist South threw down—that the ruling of the high court on civil rights was not the law of the land but the law of the case; that the Government would have to proceed state-by-state, school-board-by-school-board, voting-registrar-by-voting-registrar, Negro-by-Negro.

The first time I met members of the Kennedy family I was guest speaker at a Foundation for Retarded Children event in Boston. Mrs. Eunice Kennedy Shriver was being honored for her work in this field and she introduced me to Mrs. Joseph Kennedy and to Robert Kennedy, then counsel for the McClellan Committee. A few years later I met Senator John F. Kennedy in the Senate Office Building. He was already campaigning for the nomination for the Presidency. Senator Kennedy introduced me to Myer Feldman of his legal staff and to Ted Sorensen, his close associate.

The next time I met President Kennedy was at the White House on February 12, 1963, the celebration of one hundred years of Lincoln's Emancipation Proclamation. Almost all the civil rights leaders of the country were there. The President had not yet come to the reception when Eunice Shriver and her husband arrived.

Mrs. Shriver said, "Come with me and you may have a minute alone with him." But along the long foyer which separates the living quarters from the White House office, the

President and Mrs. Kennedy were already on the way. He greeted me warmly and introduced me to Mrs. Kennedy. And I said to her, "I hope the President isn't expecting me to march fifty miles like the Marines and the Attorney General."

The President laughed and said, "No, I'm not. Pierre Salinger started the whole thing and then quit, leaving me holding the bag of telegrams from doctors all over the country— they want to know whether I'm trying to kill the members of my Cabinet." By this time we were in midst of the reception, but I did indeed have the minute alone.

I saw him one more time, on June 21, 1963, in his White House office. I brought with me the first chapter of my book *Mr. Kennedy and the Negroes.*

While I waited outside, John Kenneth Galbraith, foreign affairs adviser and former Ambassador to India, came out, shook my hand and said, "That's the best thing you ever wrote." I knew what he referred to. A day or two earlier James Reston of *The New York Times* had quoted a line I had written about Senator Barry Goldwater: "I always knew the first Jewish President of the United States would be an Episcopalian."

When I was ushered into the President's office, Mr. Kennedy said, "Hello—that's the best thing you ever wrote."

I showed the President the first chapter of my book and explained that I had been inspired by the several books dealing with Abraham Lincoln and the Negroes. I saw a parallel between Lincoln's Administration and his own.

Mr. Kennedy made no comment on this; he merely said that Lee C. White, his special assistant counsel on civil rights, would be available for any help I might need. We discussed civil rights for the entire fifteen minutes.

I remembered being surprised because I had no idea Mr.

Kennedy had given the matter such deep thought. But indeed he had. It was he who told me that, unlike the Irish, the Jews or the Italian immigrants who made it into the open society, the Negro needed legislation every step of the way, needed it because his color marked him as a marginal man.

Before I left, I asked the President to autograph my copy of the first chapter. This copy will go to the Charlotte Public Library, which established a Golden Collection in 1960.

The everlasting monument to John F. Kennedy and his commitment to the cause of human rights is that he accepted the challenge of the segregationist South—he told the staff of the Civil Rights Division of the Attorney General's office: "Get the road maps—and go."

This was a backbreaking effort. The lawyers changed from their morning clothes in which they argued before the Supreme Court into dungarees and slacks to walk down the dirt roads and the rural highways of Mississippi, Alabama, Louisiana, Georgia, and Florida, and they knocked on doors. They have been knocking on thousands of doors of Negro sharecroppers and farmers—"Have you ever voted? Have you ever registered to vote? How many times were you turned down? Tell us about it. Tell us about the school your children go to."

And as the reports came in, the President wrote across them, *Keep pushing the cases.*

The people seemed to sense this even though the process was undramatic and could not produce headlines.

As if by instinct people began to understand what was going on, and despite the hatred elsewhere the majority of millions of Americans loved John F. Kennedy. They loved him much as philosophers loved the Idea of the Good. Good things decay but an Idea lives on.

John F. Kennedy was an Idea to the people of the United

States. More than the man he was and the office held, he was an Idea of what we could become, what we could be, what we could achieve.

Both John F. Kennedy and the country were still in the process of *becoming*. But many of us felt we were as near the state of pure being as we had been when Abraham Lincoln preserved the Union, and Franklin D. Roosevelt preserved the country.

We owe a debt of honor and gratitude to this young man who streaked across the horizon of American history—because John F. Kennedy was the first President since Abraham Lincoln to declare publicly that racial segregation and discrimination are morally indefensible.

He was the first President to support the Negro's drive for equality by making public announcement that the security of the nation, its sacred honor, and its future were inseparable from its civil rights.

Mr. Kennedy was a man who believed in the human spirit, and the only words that do him justice at all are the words he himself spoke in tribute to a poet, Robert Frost:

"We honor a man whose contribution was not to our size but to our spirit; not to our political beliefs but to our insight; not to our self-esteem, but to our self-comprehension."

Jack Johnson

IN THE early 1930's I was clerk in a midtown New York hotel and Jack Johnson, who had been the first Negro heavyweight champion, was working in a flea circus on West Forty-second Street; and I gave him a room for the night. The next morning some of my out-of-work, nonpaying guests complained. It was my initiation into the civil rights movement.

It wasn't his own vices that did Jack Johnson in. No sir, it wasn't the drinking, the wenching, the gluttonous eating. Jack triumphed over these as he triumphed over most of his opponents.

It wasn't vice, it was the anti-vice crusade.

A Chicago judge gave Jack Johnson a year and a day for consorting back and forth across state lines with a most willing woman who said Jack had seduced her. The defense lawyer forgot to emphasize that Johnson was paying the rent for the woman's mother and sister.

Poor Jack Johnson. His own character lent credence to the charges. He was proud, arrogant, careless, often irresponsible. Jack Johnson was ill-prepared in 1910 to carry the burden of self-esteem for his entire race as Jackie Robinson was able to do a generation later.

The "Eleanor Club"

THE TRUTH about Mrs. Eleanor Roosevelt ranges from the late Dag Hammarskjöld's insight that she was a friend of the whole world, to President John F. Kennedy's statement that she was one of the greatest ladies in the history of this country. The praise that followed her while living was no less than that which mourns her death. Yet eulogies are sometimes vague and imprecise and we know there was nothing vague or imprecise about Eleanor Roosevelt.

Proof of her greatness lies in the realization that it is not too early to assess her role in history.

The segregated Negro of the South started on what he calls "freedom road" during the Roosevelt Administration. Not the President, however, but the President's wife, Eleanor, was the Negro's first "official" champion.

Early in 1934 Mrs. Roosevelt visited a famous textile city in the South, and when she saw the separate drinking fountains for "white" and "colored," she called it a "degrading system" and said the entire institution of racial segregation was un-American. She said it publicly and she kept saying it publicly, thereby giving rise to the myth of the "Eleanor Clubs." The servants, cooks, and domestics were clipping her picture out of the newspapers, and the white housewives began to whisper that the Negro women of the South were secretly joining "Eleanor Clubs."

I first "met" Mrs. Roosevelt when I was about ten years old. I recalled her years later as one of the "Christian" volunteer workers at the University Settlement house on the Lower East Side, during the great wave of Jewish immigration from 1905 to 1914. Fifty years later, in October, 1962, she asked me to fill in for a speaking engagement she had at Alfred College in New York State.

But the meeting I remember most vividly was when Mrs. Roosevelt and I met in the Chattanooga airport, both of us on our way to speak at the Highlander Folk School in Monteagle, Tennessee. The Highlander Folk School was the first interracial school in the South, a place where Negro and white social workers taught together.

Mrs. Roosevelt had just returned from Europe, and one of the newsreel clips from her trip showed Queen Juliana of the Netherlands rushing down the steps of the palace with arms outthrust to greet her. Nine days later she was in the mountains of Tennessee eating her lunch from a paper plate while she sat on a harsh wooden bench. I remember her graciously putting aside her food to take a child in her arms so a Negro mother could snap a photograph.

And so let it be revealed now that there was indeed an "Eleanor Club," an unorganized "fraternity" of millions of men and women throughout the world for whom Eleanor Roosevelt was the "living witness" that the American Dream was not really a myth.

Pope John XXIII

POPE JOHN XXIII died Monday, June 3, 1963. People as diverse as U Thant, Secretary General of the United Nations, Mayor Robert F. Wagner of New York City, and the editor of *Pravda* praised his Holiness' life and the accomplishments wrought since his ascension to the Holy See.

There is no question that he was a great and humble man, a man who hopefully wrought an influence on the peace of the world.

In all senses Pope John XXIII was a friend of the Jews. To prove his equity, one of the late Pope's first rulings was to delete from a prayer a phrase which expressed no love for the people of Israel. Excising "the perfidious Jews" from the Good Friday prayer was a warm handshake.

If, during the 1960 Presidential campaign, someone had as much as whispered that John F. Kennedy would visit the Pope of Rome during his first term of office, Mr. Nixon would have won by a landslide.

That the first Catholic President could indeed visit the Pope and have all Americans applaud heartily is the amazing story of our times, and I was surprised that so many of our editors and commentators missed that angle of it.

I remember that during the 1928 campaign Senator Tom Heflin said that a Catholic President would be taking orders from the Pope. Well, so great were the accomplishments of the late Pope John, millions of people in our country and elsewhere were actually hoping that this was true, that our President would indeed take some advice from the Pope.

That an elderly man could do this within a brief four years, actually change the image of a two-thousand-year-old institution, at least in the minds of the skeptics, is one of the most remarkable stories of our times.

Jews were not the only race of man to benefit from the breadth of Angelo Giuseppe Roncalli's vision. Had my father been living on June 3, 1963, he would have repeated his favorite phrase: "The Jews have no luck." And all of us can say of Pope John's death: "Nor does mankind."

Adlai E. Stevenson

A FEW days after Dwight D. Eisenhower defeated Adlai E. Stevenson again for the Presidency in 1956, I was in the office of Jonathan Daniels, editor of the Raleigh News and Observer, a former press secretary for President Harry Truman. Said Jonathan, "My father [Josephus Daniels] went down the line for twenty-five frustrating years with William Jennings Bryan. I think, Harry, you and I are destined to spend our generation with Adlai E. Stevenson."

But indeed how lucky we were to have Adlai E. Stevenson!

Adlai E. Stevenson twice lost to Eisenhower, twice lost to one of the greatest war heroes of history. In the mountains of West Virginia and across the plains of Kansas and in the forests of Oregon, everyone knew General Eisenhower; their

sons were serving with him or they had served with him. And
Eisenhower was the kindly father image who promised to go to
Korea and to let things take their own course in the segregationist South and to balance the budget, too. In the face of
this, Adlai E. Stevenson, comparatively unknown a month
before his nomination, garnered twenty-six million votes in
1952 "talking sense to the American people," telling them the
modern world demanded more and more sacrifice, telling them
it demanded more and more experimentation, telling them life
would never be easy as long as the Cold War lasted and
promising no panaceas for its resolution.

That twice this many millions of Americans supported him
is his supreme achievement. In many ways, there could have
been no New Frontier if there had been no Adlai Stevenson to
precede it, to fertilize with ideas the American soil.

It will be for this reason that Adlai Stevenson's influence
will be a far greater influence than that of any other defeated
Presidential candidate. Not Henry Clay, not William Jennings
Bryan, not Wendell Willkie, not Thomas E. Dewey, ever exer-
cised such lasting influence. It is true that Bryan succeeded to
Woodrow Wilson's Cabinet as Secretary of State only to resign
when Wilson drafted a particularly strong protest to the German Kaiser. It is true that Wendell Willkie worked for Franklin D. Roosevelt and authored a significant book; but his un-
timely death cut short his influence.

Stevenson succeeded to John F. Kennedy's Department of
State as Ambassador to the United Nations. Just how powerful
and all-pervading an influence Stevenson had wielded was
demonstrated after the Cuban missile crisis when reporters
Charles Bartlett and Stewart Alsop published an article in the
Saturday Evening Post that purported to be the inside story of
the Administration's planning and strategy sessions. These
journalists were critical of Adlai, charging that he had advised

President Kennedy to go soft and negotiate with the Russians for the removal of the missiles.

But the story exploded in their faces. Not only did John F. Kennedy explode it, but logic itself. No one has to overhear Administration councils under such conditions to realize men change their thinking from day to day and minute to minute. No doubt some of the men sitting in on these conferences called for war. But what was interesting is that these two journalists were charging that only the man who counseled peace was suspect.

And now I'd like to publish here for the first time that even so perceptive a man as the late John F. Kennedy was amazed by the mail which inundated the White House following the story's publication. It ran ten to one for Stevenson, and it was evident that the scare word "appeasement" did not terrify Americans; and as far as Stevenson was concerned they did not believe it anyway. God help the world on the day when a Presidential council does not have a man willing to face up to the risks of peace. I have ascertained the mail represented the opinions of every conceivable kind of American—Republican Democrat, and independent; young, middle-aged, and elderly.

There are, I suspect, millions of Americans who never voted for Stevenson who are proud to live in the same generation.

Rossini and Puccini

ROSSINI, who wrote "*Stabat Mater*," the great requiem to the Virgin Mary, lived for weeks at a time in a brothel. He was a big wine, women, and song man.

Giacomo Puccini, the composer of *La Bohème*, and some of the most heavenly tunes in all opera, was also a great ladies' man. His wife once accused him of making love to every soprano in Italy. Puccini replied, "What can I do? It is my destiny."

Tennessee Williams

I HAVE lived in Charlotte, North Carolina, for over twenty years and have traveled extensively throughout the South, and I have yet to meet any of the Southerners Tennessee Williams puts in his plays. Why that should be, I don't know, but I haven't met any of these incestuous fathers, and I am a man who looks around the corners. In these twenty years, I've met the sort of people Arthur Miller puts in his plays, which may mark me as more prosaic but which leads me to suspect that, unprolific as he may be, Arthur has ten times Tennessee's talent. You don't meet the Southerners Tennessee Williams writes about because in truth they are not people and they do not come from places. They are not even ideas. They are only impositions. Tennessee Williams is an expert at taking advantage of his audience with his dramaturgical blend of sadism, masochism, and sensationalism. His characters take the same advantage as the croaky-voiced singer on the vaudeville stage warbling about his mother being his best friend. Everyone is for Mother, the Flag, and sunshine. In the same way everyone is deeply interested in sex deviation, sadists, and insanity. But the result is the same. These things mesmerize an audience. They do not instruct, nor enlighten, nor interest.

Tennessee Williams has escaped this sort of criticism for the last fifteen years because people excuse him by maintaining he is writing symbolically. But the symbols of our age, I would suggest, are not cannibalism nor impotence nor sexual deviation but rather a man who is going to lose his job, and a man who wants to vote in Mississippi.

Jacqueline

DR. RUDOLPH STEINER, the great Austrian philosopher, said every human being is called upon at least once in a lifetime for a moment of greatness.

In the face of the most dreadful tragedy, Mrs. John Fitzgerald Kennedy set an example women down the ages, in their own times of sorrow, will strive to emulate.

Pasternak's peddler

JOSEPH PASTERNAK, the Hollywood producer, told me a story. As a young boy in Hungary, he says, he began peddling fish for the Sabbath and he was underselling an old-timer who had peddled fish in that vicinity for twenty years. The old gent hauled young Joe up before the rabbi in the days when rabbis handled litigation between Jews.

"Here is this young fellow coming along underselling me, which is not fair, because at my prices I lose money every sale I make," said the old peddler. And asked the rabbi: "If you lose money on every sale you make, how come you continue to peddle fish?"

Replied the old gent, "Well, I got to make a living, don't I?"

Dr. James Parkes

EVERY once in a while we learn of a devout Christian clergyman who has devoted his career and life in curing this amazing disease known as anti-Semitism. One such clergyman is Dr. James Parkes, a leading scholar of the Anglican Church in England.

I went to hear this noble man the last time I was in England and his ideas flow with true Christian spirit. His lecture at the time was on the "Foundations of Judaism and Christianity."

Dr. Parkes is a vigorous man, sixty-five years old, with a handsome white mane. He lives in Hertfordshire and often affects an open-necked shirt instead of the collar. His concern now is that the next wave of anti-Semitism will occur in South America, and he feels we should do more work in that area.

When someone asked him about dual loyalties, Dr. Parkes replied, "It's a poor fellow who's only got two loyalties."

Boxcar Annie

ABOUT two letters a month come here for hoboes who use my address as a drop. These are the hoboes who travel on the Southern and Seaboard routes along the Eastern Coast.

Which reminds me: I've had a letter here for several months addressed to Boxcar Annie Flaherty. I haven't heard from her and I'm a little worried. I heard Boxcar Annie did a stretch of thirty days in Covington, Kentucky; I had a subsequent report that she was seen in Cincinnati in good health and in fine spirits.

Buffalo Chuck Barth is coming down to see me. Buffalo Chuck is one of the leading writers for the *Bowery News*, which is the best of the hobo press. Recently the *Bowery News* voted the admission of Carl Sandburg, Johnny Carson, and me for their social register—the register of society's basement.

Jack Teagarden

I WAS saddened by the news that Jack Teagarden, the jazz trombonist and singer, died in New Orleans. Jack was fifty-eight years old and the paper said he died of pneumonia.

I knew Jack Teagarden in the early 1930's and even helped him over two very bad periods. In those days, alcohol was Jack's problem. I was the clerk at the Hotel Markwell on Forty-ninth Street and Broadway. Paul Whiteman played at the Paradise, a night club across the street, for two years. Bing Crosby had already left the band and Whiteman's singer was a girl named Ramona. Some of the boys in the band stayed at my hotel. My good friends were Goldie, Whiteman's assistant and trumpet player, Pingatore, the banjoist, and Jack Teagarden.

I have been an opera man all my life, and I have more or less looked down on jazz musicians and singers. Jack Teagarden changed my opinion. I listened to him talk and I listened to him play, and Jack converted me, not *from* opera but *to* jazz.

The last time I saw Jack Teagarden was somewhere in the Southeast, I've forgotten where. I was making a speech in that city about four or five years ago, and I noticed an ad in the paper that he was performing. I went backstage and he threw his arms around me. These people are very generous in their emotions and in everything else. We spent most of the night talking and he gave me an insight into Bing Crosby. Mr. Crosby is quite a man. Teagarden told me that each time alcohol got him down, and he was broke, Bing would write a meaningful note to somebody in the theatrical or broadcasting world and Teagarden would immediately be put back on the right track—and with money. I understood from Teagarden that Bing did not have a particularly special feeling for him, that it was a general practice with Crosby.

I was saddened by Jack's death, a good man and a fine artist.

Mrs. Seymour remembers

ONCE a week your mother took you for a trip on one of the old-fashioned horsecars, with the hay and the stove to keep passengers warm, and you went to Vesey Street and walked from there to the Washington Market to do the week's shopping. The butter merchants were tall men who wore white linen coats and greeted each of their customers by name. They gave all interested a small scoop with which to taste the butter in the different tubs and when you made your choice, they took a larger scoop and literally gouged the creamy butter and dumped it on a clean piece of waxed paper.

These are the reminiscences of Mrs. Elizabeth Damrosch Seymour, who is the youngest sister of the late and great Walter Damrosch. Mrs. Seymour is ninety-two today and she says she appreciates her old age because she can remember so many delights of the past.

PART 8

From King Kong to Stravinsky

Shakespeare's anniversary

WE KNOW that he was baptized on April 26, 1564, so that somewhere between April 20 and April 23, four hundred years ago, was born an Englishman who possessed what was probably the greatest brain ever encased in a human skull.

William Shakespeare's work has been performed without interruption for some three hundred and fifty years everywhere in the world. Scholars and students in every land know his name and study his work as naturally as they study their holy books—the Gospels, the Torah, the Koran, and the others.

For centuries clergymen have spoken Shakespeare's words from their pulpits; lawyers have used his sentences in addressing juries; doctors, botanists, agronomists, bankers, seamen, musicians, and, of course, actors, painters, poets, editors, and novelists have used words of Shakespeare for knowledge, for pleasure, for experience, for ideas, and for inspiration.

It is hard to exaggerate the debt that mankind owes. Shakespeare's greatness lies in the fact that there is nothing within the range of human thought that he did not touch. Somewhere in his writings, you will find a full-length portrait of yourself, of your father, of your mother, and indeed of every one of your descendants yet unborn.

The most singular fact connected with William Shakespeare is that there is no direct mention in his works of any of his contemporaries. It was as though he knew he was writing for the audiences of 1964 as well as for the audiences of each of those three hundred and fifty years since his plays were produced.

On his way to the Globe Theater he could see the high masts of the *Golden Hind* in which Sir Francis Drake had circumnavigated the globe. He lived in the time of the destruction of the Spanish Armada, the era in which Elizabeth I opened the door to Britain's age of Gloriana; and he must have heard of Christendom's great victory at Lepanto against the Turks which forever insured that Europe would be Christian. Shakespeare's era was as momentous as our own. Galileo was born in 1564, the same year in which Shakespeare was born, and only a few years before John Calvin laid the foundation for a great new fellowship in Christianity. And yet Shakespeare in the midst of these great events, only seventy years after the discovery of America, did not mention an explorer or a general or a monarch or a philosopher.

The magic of Shakespeare is that, like Socrates, he was looking for the ethical questions, not for answers. That is why there are as many biographies of a purely invented man, Hamlet, as there are of Napoleon, Abraham Lincoln, or Franklin D. Roosevelt.

We are not sure of many things in this life except that the past has its uses and we know from the history of human experience that certain values will endure as long as there is breath of life on this planet. Among them are the ethics of the Hebrews who wrote the Decalogue, the Psalms, and the Gospels of the Holy Bible, and the marble of the Greeks, the laws of the Romans, and the works of William Shakespeare. There are other values which may last through all the ages of man— Britain's Magna Carta, France's Rights of Man, and America's Constitution. We hope so, but we are not yet sure. We are sure of Shakespeare.

Ben Jonson was a harsh critic of Shakespeare during his lifetime. They were contemporaries and competitors. Jonson, a great dramatist, did not like it when his play *Cataline* had a short run and was replaced by Shakespeare's *Julius Caesar*,

which had a long run. Yet when Shakespeare died, Jonson was
moved to a eulogy which he called "Will Shakespeare":

> *Triumph my Britain,*
> *thou has one to show*
> *To whom all scenes of Europe*
> *homage owe.*
> *He was not of an age, but for all time.*

The lobster from the deep

Out in the jungle, King Kong was innocuous enough.
Of course, it is true he wanted to chew up a white virgin now
and then, but that was nothing compared to what he could
have done had he chosen. It was only when the expedition got
him back to New York that he ran amok. He wrecked New
York City, kidnapped the white virgin again, and crawled to
the top of the Empire State Building where some airplanes
machine-gunned him to his death, the King fortunately drop-
ping the white virgin before he toppled to the pavement.

This is the archetypal movie. The primeval monster always
attacks civilization at its nerve center—the city; but the city
always has within itself the resources to destroy the monster.
In fact, if the monster would let cities and white virgins alone,
he would be a lot better off.

The fillip that Hollywood has added since it inaugurated
its monster series is that now the monster comes from outer
space or is awakened by hydrogen detonations. Nowadays he
isn't interested in one white virgin; he's interested in all the
white virgins. But if the monster happens to be a vegetable

from outer space, the folks in town boil him; if he happens to be organic from outer space, the folks electrocute him; and if he happens to be immaterial from either the deep or outer space, the folks hypnotize him.

Writing such movies seems to me an interesting way to make a living; and therefore I have just mailed off to my agents, who happen to be monsters of their own called MCA, a screenplay about the lobster from the deep.

The hydrogen explosions awaken the giant lobster. The big lobster crunches ships in its claws and tears up New York harbor, flinging white virgins left and right.

But if the city contains the seeds of its own destruction, it contains the seeds of its own salvation as well. What the lobster doesn't know is that Yom Kippur is just about to end and the Jews are coming out of their temples and shules. Having made the necessary sacrifice of the fast for the Day of Atonement, the Jews are desperately hungry for Chinese food (as we conveniently call the forbidden shellfish) and they fall upon the lobster and devour him.

The extra virtue of this movie is that Hollywood can make it twice; once with the giant lobster on Yom Kippur and once with a giant shrimp on Rosh Hashanah.

Classroom prayers

VICTOR JORY, the actor, appeared as spokesman for Hollywood's "Project Prayer" before the House Judiciary Committee, holding hearings on a proposed amendment to the Constitution intended to overrule the six-to-one decision of the United States Supreme Court which outlawed the

New York Regents prayer in the public schools. Jory said he was "married to the same woman for thirty years" and that the prayers he recited in school helped him achieve this happy situation.

Catholic Bishop Fulton J. Sheen and Governor George C. Wallace of Alabama separately accused the Supreme Court of bypassing the country's elected representatives by banning official prayer in public schools.

Bishop Sheen told the House Judiciary Committee the Supreme Court, a "judicial body," has become a "legislative body."

Wallace said, "We are being manipulated by a gigantic socialistic pattern."

In the Soviet Union, as happened in Nazi Germany, the child gets all his training outside the home. Indoctrinating the child is necessary to the success of totalitarian systems.

Under our system we argue the child goes to school for an education and his parents form his religious and ideological attitudes. For Sheen and Wallace and the Hollywood "conservative" group to say, no, the school should have religious prayers, is to turn all of this upside down. Maybe they are not the "fighters of Communism" they claim to be.

The conservatives boast they are anti-Federal Government and anti-centralization, but on this position they want the government to mold the attitudes of children, as the Government molds them in Soviet Russia, if you'll pardon the expression.

On the other hand, there are many people who are sincerely concerned about this classroom prayer because of widespread propaganda which alleges that "God has been taken out of the classroom." It is therefore important to remember the clarity with which Supreme Court Justice William O. Douglas expressed the decision now under attack:

"The Constitutional prohibition against laws respecting an establishment of religion must at least mean that in this country it is no part of the business of government to compose prayers for any group of American people to recite as part of a religious program carried on by government."

I was not surprised at the Hollywood group, and I was not surprised at Governor Wallace, but I was indeed surprised at the Catholic Bishop Sheen.

The Catholics were once the mightiest champions of complete separation of church and state. This was during the time Protestant prayers and devotionals were part of the public-school curriculum.

At the Constitutional Convention held in New York in 1777, the draft of the provision which declared government shall have no part in the religious education of the children was prepared in a committee of which John Jay, William Duer, Gouverneur Morris, Robert Livingstone, and Abraham Yates were members. John Jay, an anti-Catholic, proposed that "all professors of the religion of the Church of Rome should not be permitted to hold lands in or be admitted to a participation of the civil rights enjoyed by the members of this state until they solemnly swear that they verily believe that no pope, priest, or foreign authority hath power over their allegiance. . . ."

It is only fair to say that John Jay changed his opinion later in life, but his amendment was defeated by Gouverneur Morris and Chancellor Livingstone. The rule that would have made Catholics second-class citizens probably into this century was defeated by a vote of nineteen to ten.

America led the way. The complete separation was the first experiment of its kind in history, and it was brought about by the labor of men who were determined to avoid the religious conflicts of Europe.

It is well to remember, too, that most of the Protestant fellowships, including the denomination of Governor Wallace, were once waging this same fight. The first two Methodist churches in this country were disguised as private homes. If the Anglican sheriff came to arrest them, the worshipers could hide the prayer books and pretend they were visiting a neighbor. And the Presbyterians were once forced to instruct their students in absolute secrecy, the first seminary for their clergy being disguised as "a home for the aged."

The era of the American Revolution produced some of the most noble people in the history of civilization, but actually the victory which produced religious freedom in the United States was handed to us by less dramatic personalities. What brought it (religious freedom) about, of course, was the presence of these "dissenter" sects, the Presbyterians, Methodists, and Baptists. As with all great American economic and social developments, it came to us by decisions of our courts. These people wanted it on the books. Never mind that there would not be full and complete compliance. That always comes later. Once it is *on the books* the battle is won ("all else is commentary"). The court decision that confirmed our religious freedom was the result of a case in the year 1801 in the State of Virginia. The Episcopal Church, allied to the Church of England, had received large grants of land from the British Crown. The Virginia Legislature passed a law which provided for that state to confiscate these "Crown" lands after the defeat of the British. But the United States Supreme Court declared the Virginia act unconstitutional, taking the position that the grants of land made to the Episcopal Church in that state could not be revoked; they were not "Crown" property. They were *Church* property.

In the light of world history we can see how far-reaching this decision was. No other successful "rebellion" ever respected the property rights which had been established by the former regime. And since this property belonged to a *church*, we have in this neglected "detail" of American history the alpha and the omega of our religious freedom.

The second major blow struck in America for religious freedom was also handed to us by the Court. This case occurred in the year 1822. The trustees of a Roman Catholic church in Philadelphia fired their priest and asked the bishop to send them a replacement. The bishop, after consultation with Pope Leo XII, refused to follow the instructions of the trustees. The trustees sued and the lower court upheld them. Here the appellate court voided the decision of the lower court and upheld the Church. The position of the court was that if a civil authority could drive out a priest today it could close down the church tomorrow. The decision handed down on April 30, 1827, together with the Supreme Court decision in favor of the Episcopal land grants, established the American concept of the separation of church and state.

We did not get this from France or even from England. England did not achieve this until the middle of the nineteenth century when Lord Macaulay and Mr. Gladstone fought it through. In his argument for complete freedom for all religious sects, Macaulay spoke of the great Battle of Blenheim against the French and Bavarians in the year 1704: "On the morning of the battle the Duke of Marlborough received the Sacrament with the rites of the Church of England; Eugene of Savoy, an ally, confessed to a Catholic priest; the Calvinist ministered to the Dutch army, our allies; while the Danes listened to Lutheran ministers, and by nightfall our Empire was still safe."

I have always felt that the agitation for these prescribed

innocuous prayers for the classroom is due to the accelerated pace of our secularization. The fellow plays golf on Sunday and says, "Did you see where they took God out of the classroom?" A member of the Hollywood group, actress Rhonda Fleming, made this point quite clear: "We must clarify the First Amendment and reverse this present trend away from God." Miss Fleming was not trying to be funny. She probably believes this because to her all of this is a highly convenient way to follow a lick-and-a-promise religion. So many people believe that a short innocuous prayer recited in the classroom will take care of the "God Department." That's settled, they say, and now we can go on to more pleasant tasks.

The Constitutional illegality of those prescribed prayers in the classroom means that the parents will probably have to do something about it in the home and that's what's worrying them—the bother of it all.

Nostalgia and sentimentality

"NOSTALGIA and sentimentality" are to the younger Jewish and Negro writers what the words "Hep! hep!" were to the Jews on the River Rhine in the days of the Crusaders.

Alfred Kazin, the critic, keeps repeating that certain writing is great because "the author never resorted to sentimentality." Saul Bellow, in reviewing Abraham Cahan's *The Rise and Fall of David Levinsky*, writes: "I began rather skeptically . . . I expected to find nostalgic softness." Philip Roth is merciless in blotting from his work every touch of softness, and for Norman Mailer and James Baldwin the word "kindness" does not even exist.

However, for all their antisentimentality and antinostalgia, these gentlemen still write very long books.

James Joyce wrote that sentimentality was essentially unearned emotion. It is not a bad definition but that does not say sentimentality and nostalgia don't play a part in life, or what the above writers call "the real."

I grew up among the pushcarts and the sweatshops, and I remember a particular pushcart peddler who read books all day long—standing up. When a customer approached, he often conveyed the idea that she was an unwelcome intruder. He heaved a sigh of relief when she finished her shopping. There were pushcart peddlers who dealt in stolen goods, which certainly doesn't make them sentimental characters, but there were also peddlers who read standing up.

Since all these young novelists concentrate their talents on the bad peddlers, there should be at least one writer who takes care of the fellows who read standing up. Is this not so?

What it comes down to is that so many of our younger writers seem to be terrified of affection and human kindness.

The low state of high school

WHEN New York City closed down Townsend-Harris High School, it marked the beginning of the end of the high school as a progressive force. The shuttering of Townsend-Harris was symbolic of what was going on all over the country. Townsend-Harris was an intermediary school for gifted students, accelerating the regular four-year course in three.

Instead of building a Townsend-Harris High School in every city of America, we went to the other extreme; we built beautiful buildings, country-club style but without substance. We built a social campus. Soon we will have ranch-type high schools covering vast areas, and the school boards will provide horses for the kids to get from building to building.

Today, the high school is an extended kindergarten where the last thing children are expected to undergo is some of the rigors of education; it is a playground where the children's lacks and deficiencies are hidden from them, lest their deficiencies disturb them. At the same time, the churches are worried that the children will find out people die; and the vice committees are imploring the police chief to pluck all the books off the stands because the kids might read them. Then all of us sit around and deplore children for "going steady." But the kids are one jump ahead of us. They see us eager to edit the idea of competition out of education, worship, and literature; so they go ahead and edit out the competitive and contingent elements in love.

The Revolution's last battle

YORKTOWN was not the end of the Revolutionary War. The Americans were to gain one victory more.

In 1783, negotiations for final peace and independence for the Colonies were ended. On November 10, 1783, there remained in New York the remnants of the British armies, some six thousand British soldiers. There were also four thousand civilians who were "loyalists" and who had come to New York to be evacuated with the British Fleet. The Fleet was assembled in New York harbor and it was hoped that embarkation would be accomplished by November 19. The British were to occupy the old fort at Bowling Green until noon of that day, when the American contingent would march down the Old Post Road and into the Bowery, take final possession of the Fort, and raise the American flag—which represented a "new constellation of states among nations."

Major Cunningham, the British provost marshal of New York during the war and the infamous commander of the military prison, was late and was only now on his way to board a British frigate. As Cunningham, who was a mean-dispositioned man, rode down Broadway, his eye lit upon an American flag flying from the home of Mrs. Francis Day on Lispenard Street. Mrs. Day's home was about half a block out of Major Cunningham's route, but the military agreement had been that America remain technically British until the Fort was emptied and the Americans occupied it. Mrs. Day was in technical violation. Galloping over to Mrs. Day's residence, the British major reined his horse and tugged hard at the flag's rope.

Out of the house came Mrs. Day, armed with a broomstick. The powder in Major Cunningham's wig dusted the air as Mrs. Day let him have one over the head. Two sergeants tried to restrain her. She knocked the first off his horse, swatted Major Cunningham again, and with unerring accuracy landed a bitter blow over the back of the second sergeant. Major Cunningham came back to the fight. He tried to grapple with Mrs. Day, but she let him have the broom flush across the face. The Britisher had had it. He was forced to retreat. Major Cunningham was the last British soldier to leave the Colonies, and the first to leave the United States of America.

His defeat at the hands of Mrs. Day made him the butt of many jokes and an extremely unpopular man among the good people of the Mother Country.

Computers and history

I MADE a speech a few months ago at the Carnegie Institute of Technology. Carnegie Tech, as the school is more popularly called, was founded by the steel tycoon Andrew Carnegie to train technicians for the steel industry in Pittsburgh. It has far outgrown this original purpose.

Andrew Carnegie was the only robber baron who practiced *noblesse oblige.* He stated publicly that God let him make money so he could benefit mankind. "The stewardship of wealth," he called it. While other robber barons proceeded to make millionaires out of canny art dealers like Duveen and mediocre architects, Andrew Carnegie endowed schools and libraries all over America.

A Scot, Carnegie eventually retired to a castle in Scotland which he called Skibo. The auditorium at Carnegie Tech in which I spoke is called Skibo Auditorium, and in endowing it, Carnegie made only one condition: neither prayers nor preachers should ever desecrate its interior. Something to ponder.

Something else to ponder was the seminar in which I participated. The seminar went by the name of "The Computer, Creativity, and Modern Society."

I have seen two of the giant computers industry now uses. One is at Eastern Airlines in Charlotte and it keeps track not only of how many empty seats there are on those flights at every stop, but how many seats have been sold at the next airport, what time the planes are expected to land, and when they are expected to take off. The other computer was at the Jonathan Logan Company in New York. Jonathan Logan is a garment concern and the computer knows to the exact yard how many bolts of cloth are in stock, how many dresses a store in Los Angeles will buy, how many cutters are employed, how many clerks, how many dresses must be sold to pay their salaries—in short, everything.

Yet these computers inspire no widespread protest. They have done away with the job of the inventory clerks and have, in the case of Jonathan Logan, even done away with many of the salesmen. When the adding machine first made its appearance in industry, the workers protested and there were demonstrations and even some violence in the offices which first installed them. The textile loom inspired more violence for it automated even more workers from their jobs. The textile loom inspired the Luddite Revolt which raged through England and Scotland from 1811 to 1816. Workmen smashed the machines and marched against the employers and beat up fellow workers who operated these looms. The revolt took its name from Ned Ludd, who used to smash the stocking frames.

The computer has had a quiet introduction into industry; yet it dwarfs the adding machine and the loom in its consequences. Why has it inspired no widespread labor complaint? The answer lies, I suspect, in our recent history.

There is a deeper confidence since Franklin D. Roosevelt. Despite all we hear about "federal control," there is an underlying sense of security that the United States is now committed to the welfare of its citizens. If the Federal Government had not made this commitment, the computer would have long since inspired another Ned Ludd.

The computer will process statistics, but it will never provide leadership or produce ideas. Four hundred years from now, mankind will celebrate the eight hundredth anniversary of William Shakespeare. The word "computer" may not even be in the dictionary then. There'll be something else—probably a toothbrush operated by atomic energy.

Last laugh in Luxembourg

ADOLPH HITLER was riding high when he appeared before the Reichstag to report on a letter he had received from President Roosevelt. Roosevelt's letter was addressed to the heads of each of the European states. The President was afraid Europe might be plunging toward war. He pleaded for a period of reappraisal that would surely benefit mankind.

In telling his Nazi audience about the letter, Hitler stopped and said, "The same letter he sent to me, he also sent to Luxembourg," and Hitler and the members of the Reichstag could not control their laughter; it was hysterical.

With that reference to Luxembourg, Hitler did not have to continue. Roosevelt's letter was treated with worse than contempt.

But there is an amazing irony today. Luxembourg is a charter member of the Common Market, and today one-half the world, the Communist half, is less worried about the hydrogen bomb than the Common Market.

It is worth having lived through these perilous times to the point where it is now our turn to laugh like hell—you can't make war and you can't make peace today without Luxembourg.

The Common Market is undoubtedly as brilliant and will prove as long-lasting a political innovation as the Declaration of Independence and the application of universal franchise. Whenever it is mentioned, one must mention Luxembourg, which will soon sit in judgment on the admission of Great Britain.

Luxembourg is now famous for more than having produced the Steichens: Paula, the wife of Carl Sandburg, and Edward, one of the great photographers of the world. I do not know of any more romantic or uplifting development in modern history than this wonderful situation, the moment in the not-too-distant future when Luxembourg casts the deciding vote to admit to the Common Market the United States of America.

Stravinsky and cricket

DID I not write best sellers, sweat thrice weekly over a syndicated newspaper column, and shore up any falling circulation for my own paper, I would keep my peace. I would not profess my enjoyment in Tennyson, Byron, and Kipling, in Puccini, Verdi, and Mozart. I would be ashamed of keeping my peace, but I would probably be more ashamed of admitting I couldn't grasp the other poets and musicians. But I will now say, I don't grasp them. And I don't care who knows it.

I watched with care, interest, and silence the television presentation of Igor Stravinsky's ballet, "Noah and the Flood." I had not the faintest idea what it was about. To me it looked like Gathering Nuts in May with Masks On.

After this hour of deep perturbation I came not at all reluctantly to the conclusion music is not for worrying. One newspaper gives me all the worry I want for one day, not to mention four of them, and the trials, tribulations, injuries, and diseases of grandchildren.

I stand in awe of Leonard Bernstein. He should know. If he says Stravinsky is the greatest composer of the twentieth century it must be. But I am not going to convince myself just to make Leonard's teaching any more profound. Many people must have dismissed Mozart, who was certainly the greatest composer of his century. In fact, after "Noah and the Flood," I placed Mozart's "Batti, Batti" from *Don Giovanni* on the record player and put the world back on its shelves.

Listening to "Noah and the Flood" was a lot like going to the cricket game, which I did in England. After five minutes, I figured, why should I worry about this? Luckily, the Englishman who took me to see the cricketeers brought along a bottle of bourbon, which was very clever of him, considering most Englishmen like Scotch. Unluckily, I don't have a television set which also dispenses bourbon. All it dispensed that evening of Stravinsky's "Noah" was worry.

That St. Louis boy, T. S. Eliot, wrote once that poetry (and all the arts for that matter) should be as immediate as the odor of a rose. I will say this for "Noah's Flood"—it was as immediate as an assassin's bullet or a hangman's noose. This should teach us there is a qualitative difference between immediacies. Faced with the ark, the bullet, or the noose, I incline to the philosophy of W. C. Fields: "On the whole, I'd rather be in Philadelphia."

Hot dogs for three cents

ONE of my correspondents in New York wrote me a bitter letter telling me the hot dogs at one of the resorts cost twenty cents and that they are not as good as the frankfurters of bygone days. Why she singled me out for this culinary information I cannot say. She went on to say that the best hot dogs were those sold long ago by the mobile pushcarts. They cost three cents and came wrapped in a bun overflowing with mustard and sauerkraut. But I suspect they were really wonderful, madame, because we were twelve years old. The hot dogs at the resort you complain about are also eaten by twelve-year-olds and I bet they are just as wonderful as the three-cent hot dogs were to us.

One of the marks, the incontestable evidence, of encroaching old age is the complaint about food. Telling someone about how much better the food of yesteryear tasted marks you more than a headful of gray hair.

One of my brothers told me once that he thought the food tasted better years ago. I explained to him that in the first place his tastebuds change with the years and in the second how would he know since he has always been a notorious diet addict. He looked at me balefully, saying that the diets were much, much better years ago.

There are children today who cluster like a chrysalis around the television set who will remember fondly decades from now how nourishing and delicious the old television dinners were. I suspect my generation is better off in its memories.

The meals my mother cooked were prepared with love and affection, and food may well be inanimate but all of us know anything responds to love and affection. While the modern foods are undoubtedly more convenient they are equally as mechanical.

Every man to his own changing tastebuds and every generation deserves its own synthetic memories.

The talk of nations

So-called primitive nations are primitive not because they have no language, but usually because they have too many. Ethiopia has over seventy languages and some of the African nations have virtually a different language for every tribe.

India, which is sophisticated and which has a long history of culture, lists Hindi as its official tongue, but this is but a nominal designation. The Indian universities are already discouraged because of the variety of languages in which they must teach, often with only monolingual or bilingual professors.

Making this one world is indeed a large problem.

George Bernard Shaw was able to make popular its extent. *Pygmalion*, his play about Henry Higgins transforming the flower girl Liza Doolittle into a lady, is properly played as a love story. But the Shavian truth about the play is that patterns of speech are the ultimate dictator of patterns of life.

Shaw left a large sum of money in his will to the development of a new alphabet. He wanted one separate letter for every separate sound.

This is but a start. At least if English were spelled the way it is pronounced and English-speaking people accustomed themselves to this innovation, English would be an appreciably easier language for others to assimilate.

There are philosophers who argue that all differences are essentially semantic differences. I cannot wholly subscribe to this view but many differences are semantic and many national quarrels arise out of the lack of communication.

It would not be wise to drive around in our Cadillacs with signs reading STAMP OUT SWAHILI or STAMP OUT FRENCH, but maybe we could get some stickers that read, I SPEAK ENGLISH—GOOD.

Five O'Clock Teas

WHEN I was a kid on the Lower East Side of New York, one of the things I sold from time to time was Five O'Clock Teas, a very tasty cracker. We bought boxes of them for five cents each, and I believe there were fifty in a box; and we sold them for five-for-a-penny loose. We had a little stand with a tablecloth and we laid out our Five O'Clock Teas. I usually wound up eating half the product.

In Israel there are no five o'clock teas today. The Israelis serve coffee. People tend to favor what is expensive and American. If you offer a guest tea, it is considered an insult.

In an attempt to reestablish the preeminence of tea in Jewish life, a company in Israel put on an exhibition of samovars on the occasion of opening new offices. The exhibition brought to light some samovars which my readers will find interesting.

The samovar was used in old Russia, by all classes of people, as an essential item of furniture. Every self-respecting family had one; its quality depending on the size of the family and the expected number of guests. Some were made of precious metals with artistic designs. The best-known samovars came from the city of Tula in Russia. These were of such fine quality that they passed on from generation to generation.

Some of these were on exhibit recently in Tel Aviv. But there was also one made in England, and one made in modern Soviet Russia which was heated by electricity, not the same thing at all.

Much of the social life of a family was carried on around the samovar. The pleasant warmth emanating from the samovar was conducive apparently to a warm social atmosphere and good conversation. I studied the folder of the exhibition recently held in Tel Aviv, and I found that there are two hundred varieties of tea grown in twenty-three countries. Eskimos after taking sweet strong thick tea chew the tea leaves. Burmese eat dry tea leaves flavored with fried garlic nuts and coconut milk. In Tibet they make a soup of tea leaves, to which is added yak butter and salt.

Caruso and Barrymore

ENRICO CARUSO was the most glamorous personality I ever saw and Ethel Barrymore the best actress. I miss Caruso and Barrymore on Broadway. I try to remind myself that things can't hold still because I like them, but I can't help longing for the huge personality who filled the theatre. It may be true that the present-day actors, actresses, and opera singers have more talent and are probably more literate than the actors, actresses, and opera stars of thirty years ago, more so even than Barrymore and Caruso; but their personalities aren't so big.

Part of this, I think is related directly to the subject matter of the legitimate stage. Playwrights don't seem to be able or want to edit the dross from the dramatic experience.

"The theatre is always at its lowest ebb," said George Bernard Shaw, so I hope no one takes my criticism too seriously. But the world I see on Broadway is not so flavorsome as Shaw's, witty as Molnár's, or so strongly motivated as O'Neill's. It's a world filled with worriers, with characters not so nice as the audience they entertain.

Caruso and Barrymore represent more than a crank editor's nostalgia—they represented a world in which high hope and possibility were discovered and rediscovered, and that is why their theatre was always exciting. And it was a real world, too. Nothing ever seemed so dramatic as Caruso's rising from his sick bed to sail home to Italy to die or Ethel Barrymore's immediate determination to give up the starring role of her career and join the hungry actors in the Equity strike.

The Emperor in error

THE EMPEROR of the Austro-Hungarian Empire, the venerable Franz-Josef, once advised his heir apparent, Francis-Ferdinand, about what an emperor should take seriously.

Two things no man in power should ever take seriously are 1) students who riot on street corners; and 2) women who want civic improvement. If you don't worry about them, said the emperor, they will go away.

If only Franz-Josef had warned his nephew Francis-Ferdinand about students armed with revolvers, what a happy place Austria-Hungary would now be.

PART 9

The Eleventh Lost Tribe of Israel

Judaism, Christianity, and communism

FEW Christians were worried lest the Dead Sea Scrolls refute some basic tenet of the faith. The *idea* is the important thing.

By the same token there was hardly a single protest when scholars changed the name of the Red Sea through which Moses led the children of Israel to the Sea of Reeds. No one was disturbed. It makes no difference. The *idea* is all that matters. The Idea of Judaism also is eternal.

Look at the new modern religion—communism. It has millions of adherents in Russia and China. But an ordinary speech by a second assistant can shake its whole foundation and the people start pulling plaques off the walls, reburying saints, changing the names of streets and cities, and pulling down all sorts of statues.

The Judaic-Christian civilization exists in time and not in space, and does not depend on the success of the next Five-Year Plan.

The Eleventh Lost Tribe of Israel

THE amazing element involved is that the question of who is a Jew is really decided, finally, by the vast Christian majority. I knew a little boy whose father was a Jew and his mother a Christian. He got his first black eye in a fight with a kid who called him "a Jew" the week after he made his first Communion in the Roman Catholic Church.

But the trouble with considering an anti-Semite's definition, however, is that it does not apply to the here and now. Nor does it apply to people. For the anti-Semite refuses to see the Jew as a brother human.

There is another definition in modern literature. A great novel of the twentieth century is James Joyce's *Ulysses*, whose hero is a Jew who lives in Dublin and is named Leopold Bloom. Besides Joyce, Herman Wouk, Norman Mailer, James Jones, and Irwin Shaw—the four best-selling novelists of World War II—all had sympathetic Jewish characters. Writers consider the Jew as a symbolic quality. The Jew in most of modern literature is the aberrant man of culture whom the world has denied a forum. The Jew as a symbol animates much of modern literature because it is a temptation to portray him as a figure possessed of moral strength but handicapped by political and ethnic identity. This symbol is indicative of what most novelists want to talk about—the dilemma of cultural estrangement, of homelessness, of loneliness.

This definition of a Jew is no definition at all. It is neither adequate nor inadequate. It is only a literary idea.

But there is a novelist who has come close to a working definition. Curiously, he is Arthur Miller, the Pulitzer-winning playwright whose first work was a novel called *Focus*. It was about a Christian who "looked" Jewish, had a Jewish "sounding" name, and moved into a neighborhood where he was "accused" of being Jewish. He fights this and no one really believes him and in the end he resigns himself to suffering as a Jew for no reason other than the fact that Jews suffer. Bernard Malamud's fine novel *The Assistant* makes the same point about an Italian thief who falls in love with a Jewish girl.

Malamud and Miller have hit upon a philosophic truth. And, in the last analysis, it is the sectarian philosophers who furnish the definition we need. Jean-Paul Sartre, the French existentialist, says quite simply, "A Jew is a man other men call a Jew." This definition will serve. But Professor Sidney Hook offers a more satisfying definition in his essay, "Reflections on the Jewish Question." He says, "A Jew is anyone who for any reason calls himself or is called such in any community whose practice makes note of the distinction."

I feel no resentment when a Jew writes me that he is "now" a Christian. I admit I feel a little sad, but certainly no anger. I feel a little sad because the fellow has complicated his search for identity, a need as basic as bread.

Thomas Mann portrays this longing in his character Leo Naphta. The fictional Leo loses his parents in a massacre and seeks an identity, first in Marxism, then in the Roman Catholic Church. Naphta's search for identity has its echo some forty years later in the current resistance against the Communist program to dissolve the Jewish identity within the Soviet civilization, a determined resistance, despite absence of synagogue and ritual. It is hardly a coincidence that Zionism too was led by assimilated Jews—Theodor Herzl, Max Nordau, and Louis D. Brandeis.

Recently *Look* magazine ran an article about intermarriage between Gentile and Jew. Judaism may be losing seventy percent of the children born to mixed couples. There are Jews who are worried about this. But it is not a new worry.

When Napoleon opened the ghettoes of Europe in 1805, there were rabbis who bewailed the vanishing Jews who would be swallowed up by the Gentile society.

My mother, a pious woman, worried about the vanishing Jew in 1910. She felt we would all become "Americanized" and lose our faith and our identity.

But the Jew did not vanish after 1805, nor after 1910, nor will he vanish after 1964 nor after 1994.

Christians have no intention of letting the Jew do a vanishing act.

Look magazine does not fret alone. The Commission on Jewish Affairs of the American Jewish Congress recently sponsored a conference on the marriage between a Gentile and Jew.

Rabbi Leo Jung of the Jewish Center in New York said: "Intermarriage . . . is unfair to the Jewish people, past, present, and future; it is unfair to the non-Jew; it is unfair to the institution of marriage."

Rabbi Joseph Klein of Temple Emanuel in Worcester, Massachusetts, said: "Most Jewish parents, even those who are lax in their religious observance, regard the marriage of their child to a non-Jew as a calamity . . . they are completely beaten in their arguments if there is a rabbi in the community who is known to solemnize mixed marriages."

Rabbi David Eichhorn of the National Jewish Welfare Board said: "We shall need the forbearance of Moses, the wisdom of Solomon, and the patience of Job to solve all the problems that have come upon us and will continue to come upon us because of the gradually increasing number of religiously mixed marriages in the United States of America."

To this last, I must say, God help us because Moses, Solomon, and Job have apparently thrown it in our lap.

To Rabbi Klein, let me say there are always parents who exert pressures to prevent marriages mixed or not. Wise children pay no attention. Nothing calms parents and dignifies them and uncalamitizes them like a grandchild.

As to Rabbi Jung, I say he certainly has placed a heavy burden on the young who marry, whether they marry Gentiles or Jews. Does anyone take a mate with the idea of playing fair with the past, present, and future of the Jews?

We Jews, no more than anyone else, cannot have it both ways. We cannot live in a pluralistic society with the guarantees of religious freedom and keep inviolate all our religious traditions and mores.

<u>What has always made me smile is the observation of the many Jews who wage desperate war to join the Gentile country club and at the same time insist other Jews not marry Gentiles.</u>

What I think everyone misses in the dialogue on mixed marriages (although Rabbi Klein seems somewhat aware of it) is that religious ritual itself is not enough to insure absolute generic perpetuity.

I was sitting in the lounge of a jet returning home from Israel not too long ago, and I chanced into a discussion with a great philanthropist. He is an American-born Jew who has devoted his time and energies and a good portion of his wealth to Israeli charities. Something about Israel, however, dismays him. He told me sadly, "They don't go to *shul*. I've never seen anything like it. They don't go to *shul*."

I told the philanthropist not to burden his heart with worry about the Israeli non-*shul*-goers. After all, there is a difference between him and the Israeli. The philanthropist lives in a suburb and when he rises in the morning he needs *identity*. For the philanthropist's banker does not consider him simply a suburban developer. At the luncheon table in the City Club, his banker says to his friends, "I have some of the best Jewish business in town." Nor does his lawyer consider him simply a client who is a graduate engineer turned land developer. His lawyer tells colleagues during a bull session at the convention in Honolulu, "Our office has been getting most of the Jewish business in recent years."

My philanthropist needs to confirm the *identity*. To satisfy this need, and because of the social segregation which sets in after sundown each day, he needs to pile one activity atop the other until the temple becomes the center of his sociological being. Thus, he creates the criterion that this participation is the basis of being a Jew.

I've visited with Bernard M. Baruch three or four times.

"Does he go to *shul?*" people ask me, as though somehow Baruch would cease being Jewish if he didn't. Invariably, the fellow who asks, "Does Baruch go to *shul?*" attends *shul* himself perhaps three times a year. But he needs Baruch in the *shul* every Sabbath to add greater dignity to his *identity.* So too does he need the Israeli to go to *shul*—more so, in fact. But the Israeli is already in *shul.* When he gets up in the morning he has no compulsion to prove anything nor does he need to pride himself on this. They have deserts to irrigate and borders to patrol and trees to plant. The whole country is a *shul.*

The Israelis, in short, aren't troubled by ambivalence; they know what they are. Businessmen are simply businessmen in Israel and writers are writers. The rest of the world is populated by businessmen and Jewish businessmen and books are written by writers and Jewish writers.

There are those who are secure in their Jewishness who never worry whether Bernard Baruch goes to *shul* or not.

They also do not worry about "the vanishing American Jew."

But let us not minimize the importance of our one ace-in-the-hole—the Christians. The Christians dare not let us vanish. We are the "living witnesses." The Roman Catholic burial service, ". . . into the bosom of Abraham," would have no meaning if there were no Jews, and the Protestants look forward to the Biblical fulfillment: "Ten men out of all languages of the nations shall take hold of the hem of him that is a Jew, saying, we will go with you, for we have heard God is with you."

Without us there can be no Second Coming of Jesus. Christians are not unmindful of this.

Causerie on Germany

THERE were three-piece German bands that toured the Lower East Side and played German folk tunes. Our mothers rolled up pennies in bits of newspaper and threw them into the street. We identified the Germans with their singing. Sometimes we walked up through the German district and stood outside their cafés and it was very pleasant to hear the songs.

These attitudes were strengthened by the pro-Germanism of the immigrant Jews. This pro-Germanism derived from the prestige the German Jews had won. These German Jews were the greatest advertisement Germany ever had. The Jews who came to America between 1880 and 1920 cut their ties with Hungary, Poland, Russia, Austria, Latvia, Roumania, and Lithuania. They looked back upon their departure from ghetto and Pale of Settlement with considerable relief. Not the German Jews. Along with other Americans of German origin, they maintained cultural ties and expressed their affection for the "Homeland."

Thus the crime of betrayal was to be added to that of mass murder. In killing the Jews the Nazis also murdered the most ardent of all German patriots.

Before World War I we were aware that Germany had produced many socially advanced ideas—universal education, medical insurance, social security, and a social-democratic political party. Great philosophers appeared to break through the taboos of the Victorian Age. German music reached such heights that only "miraculous" can describe it—the liberation in Beethoven's Fifth, the tenderness in Brahms, the romanticism in Franz Schubert, and the fulminations of the old gods that Wagner gave us. Wagner seemed a charming echo of a long-dead pagan world of petty gods and their small enmities that hadn't really existed in the first place.

The first inkling that it might be real was easily explained away. After all, if one accepted an invitation to sing at a Natur Klub and the audience was entirely nude, was it not the new impatient casting aside of conventions? Some German ladies who lived alone had never gone to sleep without rolling a ball under the bed to watch it come out on the other side. These inhibitions went. Mendelssohn no longer appeared on the concert program. Heine with his depth and shrewd insight was no longer quoted. It was hard to determine from whence came this breeze which was to fan the greatest massacre in all the history of mankind.

Some went along with this for a little while cherishing the old values and listening to the new musicians, new poets, and new philosophers. This peace ended when the new musicians, the new poets, and new philosophers produced works of sickening perversion. At one time these would have been laughed off in a Germanic gust of good cheer, but the delicate balance of reality had been lost in World War I. In the war's aftermath the Germans took the perversion to their hearts.

The truth of the matter is that Germany could not live with herself in defeat. This was the essential defect in her national character. Nothing in her past could help her; she was too young. France had learned how to live with defeat, then with victory. Britain had learned to lose battles yet win wars and had become a master at political science. Germany could not accept world events when they waylaid her in her march to what she considered her proper place in the sun. Tragically she proved that she was unworthy by developing no inner resources equal to her ambition.

The smoldering tribal fires were all she had left and these she fanned. She could go back fifteen hundred years and the hurts of today would not exist. For many a German Jew, it was like watching one's parent go insane day by day. Panic came and then mental palsy. Perhaps now Germany felt if she regained her pristine Teutonic totality, that would be her strength and her victory. She could go through gnawing at the very flesh of her bones, if by so doing the ancient tribal gods would make her as she had been and not as she had become. But the gods were really dead after all. And now we must remain forever frightened of the people who followed a dead god.

I would guess it will take many years of education to turn Germany's passive and formal democracy into an active one on the American or British plan. The Japanese will become democratic much quicker, since the atomic bombs dropped on Nagasaki and Hiroshima obliterated all guilt. But the Germans had no alleviating agent. There is every reason to hope the Germans will turn themselves into a democracy. The Bonn Government does not intend to be an interregnum government between dictatorships as the Weimar Republic was. The difference between the two is that in the Bonn Republic, democrats hold power in every important field. In the Weimar Republic where the democrats were vocal, no one listened.

Germany's eternal struggle has been between Goethe and Hitler; between Beethoven and Eichmann.

Wisdom of the Navajo

WHILE visiting the University of New Mexico where I spoke to the student body, I uncovered this story about one of the great American Indian tribes.

Both the Navajos and the Cherokee Indians were pushed

into the desert until, early in the twentieth century, oil began to spout from the desert floor. Still later, uranium became important.

The Cherokees and the Navajos were sitting right on top of both. When the big dough came in, the Cherokees split the money up among themselves and a whole lot of them bought Cadillacs or had thirty telephones installed.

The Navajos, on the other hand, declared the money a tribal fund. No individual got his hands on any of it. They built dams and began to irrigate the desert lands. From these farms, more funds flowed in and from these they began to go into the motel business.

The Navajo money does not lie idle. Twenty million dollars a year goes into a scholarship fund for Navajo youth. Young Navajos are a high proportion of the students at the university in Albuquerque.

The Navajo considers his name sacred, part of his soul. He does not banter it around like a Texas Rotarian. A tourist asks his name, the Navajo looks at the stranger, thinking how much he can take, and answers, "Me Chief Sit-on-the-Mountain." If the tourist appears impressed the Navajo presses the advantage and like Jack Benny, milks it dry; ". . . and my cousin's name is Prince Spit-in-the-Rain," etc., etc.

The Navajos do not have television. After the evening meal the families sit around the table and entertain themselves by repeating what they had told the tourists during the day. You hear a sudden burst of laughter from out of one of the open windows, you hear a loud voice; ". . . and then he told him his sister's name is Princess Go-in-Backwards."

These Indians also have a showplace called Window Rock Tours and the profits from these tours also help supplement scholarships.

In addition, it is the Navajos who provide some of the cultural features for this section of our Southwest. It is they who import Harry Belafonte and the New York City Ballet and the touring operatic and concert companies.

How many people in our civilization today have the wisdom of the Navajo?

Chinatown

ONCE upon a time, the safest place in New York City was Chinatown. There were a lot of myths about joss houses and the opium dens, the tong wars and the slave trade, but rumors they were. The rumors circulated perhaps because Chinatown was so law-abiding, because its social structure was highly stratified and absolute. It was a place where children respected fathers and fathers respected tradition.

According to a recent report, this is no longer true. Where once there was no juvenile delinquency, now authorities momentarily expect the appearance of juvenile gangs just as happened in the Chinatown in San Francisco.

Chinatown used to be not only a self-sufficient community but also a self-regulating one.

But the problems of the Cold War, the anxiety over nuclear testing, the worldwide revolt of the have-not nations—all of these have diminished the strength of the family unit. Fathers know they cannot cope with them and knowing this they lose heart and find they cannot cope with their children. For most Americans this knowledge has been an incipient growth; for the Chinese, no doubt, it is a sudden malignant blossom.

The robes of office

IT IS no coincidence that North Carolina was the last state in the Union to ask its judges to don the traditional black robes. The Calvinist tradition goes very deep. From 'way back it frowned on the "robes of office" with a suspicion that can be traced to its struggle with the Papacy. This North Carolina was the original land of the buckskin boys—the fellows with the rifle, the ax, and the bag of corn—and there had better not be any adornments in the church, not even a vase of flowers.

The judicial robe goes back to the Hebrew priesthood. John Selden, the English lawyer who lived in the early part of the sixteenth century, introduced the robe for the judiciary. A great student of Hebrew and Catholic Church law, Mr. Selden adopted the robe idea for the bench, an idea which the Catholic clergy had borrowed from the Jewish priesthood. Pope Hildebrand had advised, If you want to rule over people you must make yourself as unlike them as possible. Mr. Selden saw the need of this respect transferred to the bench. You hand down a judgment that may mean life or death to a prisoner before the bar and somehow the prisoner himself feels better about "the robe." It is much better than being sentenced to the gas chamber by a fellow in a Hart-Shaffner and Marx suit.

The Irish and marriage

THIS old gent I knew in Jersey City was eighty-four. He had made a fortune in hauling and draying and he lived with his daughter Maureen—rather, she lived with him—and, said he, he had never seen the man good enough for Maureen; but when the right man did come along he would gracefully step aside and let Maureen become a bride. Maureen was sixty-one when I knew her and raised canaries, parakeets, and had a pet monkey. All the people at St. Aloysius parish where we lived said that Maureen was a fine girl. Any unmarried Irishwoman who is not a nun is a girl.

An Irishman writes me that he is intrigued by an essay in one of my books, "Why Irishmen Don't Marry."

Even today there are countless Irishmen and women among the Boston Irish who just never begin dating and who remain celibate throughout their lives. These are often very attractive and well-adjusted people who could easily find a mate. (It is not only in Ireland that this happens, but wherever the Irish settle.) In countless Irish families in Boston there are three to five single adult siblings still living together in their childhood home. None of them ever had a reason for leaving. It is also interesting that the Irish of both sexes, in spite of late marriage or no marriage at all, rarely indulge in sexual dalliances. They simply abstain.

The Irish family is nearly always a matriarchy. Thus in the matriarchal Irish home the women are strong, self-sufficient, bright, capable, with self-confidence and great inner resources. Herself, she grows up feeling superior to men, considering them mostly a problem and a burden. According to her particular nature she tends to dote on them, mother them, baby them, put up with them, push them, excuse them, bully them, and direct them.

And all of this has made him a bit timid where women are concerned, but a lion when it comes to holding up his own with male adversaries.

Research on the lone Jew

IN MY book *For 2¢ Plain*, I said that the best job in the world was that of being the lone Jew in a small Southern town. To his Gentile neighbors, the lone Jew becomes "our Jew" and they guard him as respectfully as they guard the Confederate monument.

Dr. Edward Martin Block, of Lexington, North Carolina, held such a job. A practicing physician there since 1939 and coroner of the county since 1955, he recently died at fifty-seven.

The entire populace turned out for his funeral. The stores closed and school let out, since it was for many children an educational opportunity: it was the first chance they had to see a real, live rabbi.

Dr. Block, like all the lone Jews in the small Southern towns, provided his neighbors with a tie to history and represented for them the living witness of the Second Coming.

Though I have studied this phenomenon at close range for many years, I am still unable to pinpoint at what figure all of this changes. There is a moment when the Confederate monument becomes much more important than the Jew, who is no longer "our Jew." I don't know whether this happens when there are eight Jews, eleven Jews, or thirty-seven Jews, but it is somewhere along in there that the change does indeed take place. As soon as I figure out the exact number, I'll let you know.

Chess players and violinists

WHY are the champion chess players Jewish? And the violinists?

The chess players in the United States include the two champions Reshevski and Fischer. In the Soviet Union also the three champions are Jewish—Betvinik, Boleslavski, and Smislov. The Hungarian champ, Szabo, is a Jew and so is the Argentinian, Neudorf.

Did the one-hundred-and-fifty-year experience in the European ghettoes encourage speculative thinking? Or perhaps the need to be ready always with some plan of escape?

But what about the violinists? Except perhaps for Zino Francescatti, all the great violinists, past and present, were Jews—Elman, Kreisler, Zimbalist, Heifetz, Menuhin, Szigeti, Millstein, Isaac Stern, and, of course, Oistrach.

Even the two best-known female violinists are Jews, Erica Morini and Ida Haendel.

Pablo Casals tried to explain it. He said Jews possess the patience and the inbred toughness to produce great musicians. He added reflectively, "I am probably the only great instrumentalist in the world who is not Jewish."

Nathan Millstein, too, has tried to explain it: "In the ghettoes of eastern Europe, the Jews studied the violin because when they had to run for their lives, it was easier to pick up a violin than a piano."

All of which means that the ancestors of the great Jewish artists of the piano—Josef Hoffman, Rubinstein, Horowitz, and Serkin—were greater optimists than the forebears of Stern, Millstein, Heifetz, Elman, Menuhin, and the others. Is this not so?

These Hungarians

SOMEONE should write a monograph on the particular genius of the Hungarian Jews.

Among the scientists there was the late Dr. Von Neumann, the late Dr. Theodore Von Karman, Professor Szilard, and, of course, Dr. Teller of hydrogen-bomb fame.

Among the best American conductors are included Riener, Ormandy, and Szell.

There was a time when Hollywood was under the spell of the Hungarian Jews. Cukor was a leader in the film colony, and Pasternak, who was recently a guest in my house, is still producing.

Rozsa composes beautiful film music and Mike Curtiz did a great job with *Life with Father*. (Mr. Curtiz had a plaque on his wall which warned: *It's not enough to be a Hungarian*.) And gifted writer Ferenc Molnár.

Interestingly enough, the founder of modern Zionism, Theodor Herzl, also was born in Budapest.

As a matter of fact, they might have very well conquered the entire intellectual world, these Hungarian Jews, except for two things: their accent and their trouble in using revolving doors.

Jewish converts soar

A SUBTLE drama has been transpiring at the Dhahran Air Force Base in Saudi Arabia. Over the past two years, at least eleven members of the United States Air Force have become converts to Judaism. Four others have indicated their intention to marry Jewish girls and become Jews.

What is behind this?

The airmen in the service call the Dhahran Air Base in Saudi Arabia the "air-conditioned hell." The word is out that this is about as bad a place to pull a hitch as any in the world. Apparently a few American airmen have found a way out.

The Arabs prohibit Jewish personnel in Saudi Arabia, which is a great insult to the Flag and to the dignity of the United States of America, but it is certainly a favor to Jewish boys in the Air Force.

Since the Air Force keeps complete records on all its men, it is impossible for a Christian boy to tell his commanding officer he cannot go to Saudi Arabia because he's Jewish.

So some of the airmen, once posted, have friends back home or in West Germany mail them a Mazuzah and a Star of David. The recipient makes certain the Arab cleaning in the shower room sees these symbols of Judaism dangling from his neck.

In a day or two, the post commander sends for the airman. "What are you trying to pull here with that Star of David?" asks the officer. "You're a Baptist from Greenwood, South Carolina. What are you trying to pull?"

"Yes, sir," says the airman. "I am a Baptist from Greenwood, South Carolina, sure enough. But not for long. I'm engaged to a Jewish girl and intend to become converted." A week later our friend is transferred to the base at Frankfurt, Germany, where there is no Prohibition and no misery.

A Jewish officer in Washington, assigned to find out why so many Baptists, Methodists, Presbyterians, Episcopalians, and Roman Catholics have so suddenly declared their intention to become Jews, observed that Congressmen trying to amend the defense treaty with Saudi Arabia are doing a disservice to Jewish boys. If the amendment passes, Jews will be qualified to serve at Dhahran, and Judaism will lose many new converts.

Latin honesty

WHEN a Latin American looks at a woman, he frankly looks at her. He smiles and stares.

An American who sees a pretty woman shifts his eyes to something else, but manages to keep the corner of his eye focused on the beauty. He is a hypocrite. This has been very bad for America and I think it is this sly habit that has gotten us the reputation of having a lot of female impersonators. I doubt that women admire this trait. Some day we will achieve the Latin directness of being able to look at a woman and keep looking, and looking, and looking.

PART 10

More Complaints and Free Advice

How to read a book, and why

READING is a joy, but not an unalloyed joy. Books do not make life easier or more simple, but harder and more interesting.

Reading is a partnership. Like any partnership, you get as much out of it as you put into it. Some partnerships are profitable, some just dead horses. Unlike most partnerships, however, reading is not the sort of joint venture which must show profits nor does it even have to chart its volume. One book a year is sufficient—provided it is the right book; and by the right book I mean a book the reader understands and assimilates.

I would like to consider why we Americans do not wish to enter into the partnership. The truth of the matter is, we do not read books. It is true we publish more books than ever before, but this is not an encouraging sign, considering the books. Half are "self-help" books dedicated to teaching people how to feed a husband, set a table, play bridge, or turn a neurosis into a profitable occupation, and another third are "nothing" books, memoirs of the celebrity or starlet who is "hot" at the moment.

There are several reasons why we do not read, and chief among them is the fact that we are poorly educated. For too long we have been trying to educate our children on the charity of underpaid teachers; and, as a consequence, our teachers are no better than they have to be. Teachers do not find time to deal with the world of literature, only with the required reading list on the absurd daily-lesson plan. Even our colleges rarely produce bilingual graduates the way every grammar school in Europe does.

Another reason advanced for not reading is that we haven't time. Translated roughly, this probably means that science has overcome us with the affliction of gadgetry and the economy with the affliction of compulsive buying, both of which do consume time and conspire to keep the better part of ourselves from influencing the poorer part.

Neither the English yeoman nor the Midwestern pioneer had much time for schooling. Both, however, could quote chapter and verse from the Bible. Once every Jewish peddler knew every gloss in the Mishnah. But few Jews and few Christians today know their Book.

The overpowering reason why we do not read is that we are losing faith in the future and in ourselves.

If nothing else, reading is an affirmation of the future by an ability to use the past.

One has only to consider the size of the industries created by the invention of television and tranquilizers to realize that a large part of the American public is intent on shutting up the mind. A nation narrowing its attention does so because it is frightened—frightened because it suspects there may well be some insoluble problems.

Reading may not necessarily solve all problems, but it teaches one how problems were faced in the past. The suburban husband who reads Dickens' *Oliver Twist* on the 8:12 might get the idea there are such things in this world as degradation and want and poverty and he might reason that the rest of the commonwealth may not resemble his clean, well-kept suburban street. He may even close the book with the realization that there is very little he can do about it, but the knowledge that something ought to be done is the first step.

"Don't teach me the answers," said the first great philosopher, Socrates. "Just find me the questions. If I know the questions, I will make it a better world."

The discovery of *the question* is the great bonus reading confers, but we seem to lose the ability to decipher questions. We seem to comprehend only imperative sentences.

Please do not confuse my cynicism with my own love of books and, I might add, my understanding of the role books have played in the progress of our civilization and in our daily lives.

When you read you are really thinking with minds of genius, of experience, and minds without fears.

Reading properly helps you to become a self-thinker. No one ever did a considerable piece of work in this world who was not a self-thinker.

The people who helped encourage our anti-intellectualism are the same people who resent self-thinkers. History shows that the best government was conceived by the self-thinkers, the literary men. Benjamin Franklin was probably the number-one philosopher of his time. Thomas Jefferson had read everything of consequence. Alexander Hamilton was a great intellectual and so was James Madison. John F. Kennedy was a reader who made notations on his books as every self-thinker does. So was Woodrow Wilson. Across the Atlantic, the greatest accomplishments were made by the literary men—Disraeli, Gladstone, Balfour, Churchill.

Alexander the Great went looking for the literary man and when he found Diogenes at Corinth, he said, "Were I not Alexander, I would wish to be Diogenes."

Caesar was a literary man. His *Commentaries* were not excelled until Winston Churchill. Both made history and then wrote about it.

Napoleon was a literary man, probably one of the greatest readers of his time. Wherever he went, he tried to spend as much time as possible with learned men. Lord Rosebery in his biography of Napoleon says that the conqueror had a library of eight hundred volumes on the field with him at Waterloo.

There is no substitute for reading.

I have discussed two topics which bring me unabating mail. One is audio-visual education and the other is rapid reading. Everyone presumes I have condemned both out of hand—a misconception far from the truth.

I said nothing mean about the true values of the audio-visual method properly applied. What I did say was that I saw evidence that audio-visual materials were used as a substitute for reading books. Many adherents of the audio-visual revolution maintain stoutly that, indeed, audio-visual techniques can reproduce books. All I maintain is that there is an intimate relationship between the mind and the printed page, between the eye and the words, which no mechanical technique can ever equal.

The psychological advantages of privacy are complex advantages. Reading and imagination, creativity and speculation are the ultimate champions of the unfettered mind and they only unfetter the mind in the uninhibited areas of privacy.

"Mind, mind has mountains," wrote the poet Gerard Manley Hopkins; and I suspect these mountains are never scaled in the formality of group attention and group efforts, which is not to say we must dispense with the audio-visual techniques. It is to say we must not overvalue them.

There are many others who write me testifying to their own reading improvement after they completed "rapid reading" courses. I have no doubt these folks are sincere and no doubt that they have improved their reading rate. Rapid reading is fine for reading a Wall Street brochure or for scanning the newspapers or business reports. It may even be okay for a James Bond thriller by Ian Fleming. But it will never do for Don Quixote.

Browse through the library of any writer or exemplary teacher and you will find the leaves of the book dog-eared and scribbled notations in all the margins. No one interested in what an author is saying should read without pencil in hand.

I defy anyone to rapid-read Homer's *Odyssey*. I defy anyone who reads it not to pause with exhilaration when Odysseus sees again, the "smoke rising from the hearths of his native land."

The Irish novelist James Joyce said of his *Finnegans Wake* it took him twenty years to write it and he expected it would take good readers twenty years to read it. One of the great American critics and writers, Austin Warren, said he could read Immanuel Kant or Aristotle at night, but his mornings had to be reserved for Dostoevski or Samuel Butler when his mind was at its most alert.

Rapid reading, too, has its virtues, but we must not fall victim to the book club advertisements which insist people at parties discuss literature. As anyone who has been to a party knows, they discuss baby formulas and capital gains.

I was fortunate to have acquired the habit of reading when still a very little boy. And once you acquire this habit you begin to absorb words the way a sponge takes water, and the results are just as refreshing.

Thousands of students write me about books. I tell them all of this and explain that the great book selections I would make are irrelevant and immaterial. They can make selections of their own and they shouldn't take my selections as absolutely necessary. The big point is to read and to become a self-thinker, to read with a pencil in your hand. While I still insist that these selections are matters of personal preference, there are some books which are necessary for the cultivated mind and educated man—the Bible and Shakespeare, and Hume's *History of England*, Homer's *Iliad* and Cervantes' *Don Quixote*, and the *Autobiography of Benjamin Franklin*, and Gibbons' *Decline and Fall of the Roman Empire,* and Henry George's *Progress and Poverty,* and Lecky's *History of European Morals* and Plutarch's *Lives.* Henry Thomas Buckle's *History of Civilization in England* I consider of particular value. Keep Emerson's *Miscellanies* at your side, and Carl Sandburg's one-volume *Lincoln.*

I have in mind hundreds of others which are of equal importance, and that's the danger of trying to select any list of books. But build your own inventory. Once you've formed the partnership, you can never again be poor.

Let's hedge the space bet

THE space program frankly is a gamble. It is gambling billions of dollars that there is something useful in space. Maybe not.

I do not mean we ought to abandon this program. By all means let us go to the moon; let us go to Mars and Venus for that matter. But let us hedge on this bet, too. There is no reason why we have to "go for broke."

If we appropriate one billion dollars for the exploration of the ocean floor we will collect on a sure thing. The wealth on the ocean floor is unimaginable. Not only could we recover sunken gold, but it is very possible that unheard-of minerals exist in quantity there.

The French exploded their atom bomb in the Sahara Desert but they are also experimenting with the ocean and displaying considerable vigor.

To give you an idea of what wealth we might accumulate were we to institute a similar ocean program, we have but to recall that in 1907 one of the Roman Emperor Tiberius's ships was reclaimed as a wreck off the coast of Tunisia after nineteen centuries. The ship contained sixty marble columns from the quarries in Attica and a cargo of works in bronze and marble which had apparently been repaired. The Emperor had probably dispatched these treasures to craftsmen in Africa and the ship went down in a storm on its return trip.

No museum has ever set a price on this art because its worth is incalculable. The ocean floor has a greater wealth than exists anywhere else in the world. It probably also has the secrets of where we came from and maybe even can tell us why we are here.

Who owns TV?

EVERY day the dialogue between Americans reproduces some of the most inaccurate assumptions. Not even the witch doctor who stuck needles in wax puppets was more misguided. I get countless letters from people saying, "Television programming is a crying shame, particularly when you consider that the people own the airwaves."

The people do not own the airwaves. The people who televise—NBC and CBS and ABC—own the airwaves.

I believe the canard of public ownership has been circulated by the broadcasters themselves. If they convince people they own the airwaves, the people will keep tuning in on their programs. The people are in the position of the farmer who watched the squatters moving in for the last seven years and kept telling himself they would leave when he wanted to use the front lawn for grazing ground. The newspapers have been much more forthright. This is a *Hearst* paper. This is a *Scripps-*

Howard newspaper. This is one of the *Knight* papers. No nonsense about the public *owning* the press.

Another piece of dialogue that gets taken seriously is that time is worth money. Salesmen are always the most adept at this. They try to sell me every mechanical piece of tomfoolery with the reasoning that there are many things I shouldn't do myself—like make carbons—because my time is worth money. Time isn't worth money, only the time you work. Anyone who tries to utilize the entire twenty-four hours in a day will find that sanitariums cost money.

There's a sort of a Gresham's law in operation here. The guy that says time is worth money is the fellow who spends three hours at lunch. And the people who say they own the airwaves are the ones who, given six programs, each a little worse than the other, will watch the very worst.

I miss the family fight

ONE of the joys of which all of us are now deprived by Madison Avenue's togetherness campaign and the invention of the one-story ranch house is the family fight.

I know people who live in perpetual annoyance with each other. They say of each other that they are selfish or egotistical or immature, but they don't seem to be able to come to grips with anything but this jargon. The last nasty word I heard a husband and wife exchange was at the opera thirty-five years ago and he called her a "dumbbell" at which she flounced out.

This inability to speak precisely extends even into politics. Once upon a time a Senator said of Henry Clay that "like a dead mackerel in the moonlight, he shines and he stinks." But listen to a couple of Senators disagreeing nowadays and you'd think they were arguing how to play cricket rather than charging one another with fiscal irresponsibility.

Robert Welch, who founded the Birch Society, called unfortunate publicity upon himself when he called Dwight D. Eisenhower a Communist. Unless you charge a man with immaturity, Communism is the worst accusation you can make. So don't let anyone tell you Freud and Marx haven't invaded our lives completely.

I long for the days when we had election slogans like, "Blaine, Blaine, the continental liar from the State of Maine," and a husband with enough courage to call his wife a "birdbrain."

Everything's the best

Ask a fellow how he likes his little foreign car and he will answer, "By golly, you ought to buy one of these. I get one hundred forty-three miles to the gallon and the car isn't as small as it looks. Why, last summer I took the wife, the wife's mother, the three kids, and the maid out to see the Grand Canyon in absolute comfort." He has neglected to tell you the car rarely starts, and that it needs a new battery every eight hundred miles, but he has appeared well-informed and positive.

Americans dispense information graciously, promptly, and generously. That it happens to be wrong information shouldn't obscure their motive which is pure.

Every city or town you visit is the world's best; every doctor you ask about is the best doctor; every dentist the most reasonable. Invariably the doctor recommended spends the whole consultation period declaiming on the evils of Medicare and then ships you off to a specialist to have the splinter from your finger removed.

No one ever has the raw guts to say, "I don't know a responsible baby-sitter," or "I can't recommend you buy that house because it leaks and is haunted besides."

The one thing people won't pass out freely is an introduction to their boss when you're unemployed. But they fortunately happen to know of a dandy employment agency.

Is Marvin a dope?

HARDLY anyone understands why everything goes so smoothly for Marvin, who is a real dope, while brilliant Stanley gets involved in every snafu and has to burn the midnight oil unraveling the snarls of work at the office.

But Marvin never forgets the office girls. When he goes on trips he sends back small presents and when he is on the job he orders flowers on his way to the golf course. The girls labor long and longingly to help Marvin, human nature being what it is. When a customer asks for a salesman, the girls route the call to Marvin, and he is considered the firm's most promising employee. He may not be such a sap, after all.

How to win the pennant

THE pitcher is the key to baseball success. No matter how much power you have in your batting order, if your pitchers allow an average of six runs per game to the opposition, you will lose six games out of nine. If your pitchers allow

only three runs per game to the opposition clubs you will win
seven games out of ten and the pennant.

Teachers need prayer

PITY the teachers who will miss the daily prayers, miss
them much more than their students.

It was during the brief pious beginning of each day that the
teacher fervently and silently asked God to help her through
another day at this ranch house the community calls a school.

She reminded God she spent years in college and in training
for which the local community rewarded her with two thousand dollars a year less than the mayor's secretary or the unionized pipe-fitters. She also reminded Him how vulnerable she
was to the assaults of the parents and how often her dinner was
interrupted with phone calls from people who demanded to
know why Johnny got a "C" when he can't read.

The prayer helped her through the daily trivia demanded by
neurotic parents, sanctioned by school boards, and encouraged
by bureaucrats who wanted to develop the "whole" child.
Once the "whole" child didn't do the job, the teacher was
confronted by the whole family, eager to work off its tensions.

The teachers will miss the prayers.

The ugliest word

UNTIL lately I had always supposed the word "victuals"
was the ugliest word in the English language. What changed

my mind were the reports from the winter Olympics. I found a word uglier than victuals. The word is "slalom." It is an exercise skiers perform on a hill, I think. It is an awful word, as slippery and unpleasant as castor oil.

The lazy words

The English language has several dozen ugly words like "dichotomy" and "bifurcation" about which we can do nothing since they already mean (I believe the professional semanticists say "signify" or "connote") something. We certainly make no improvement when we infest the language with our lazy words—words like "gimmick" which does not even mean, connote, or signify much of anything at all. "Give me the picture," the boss asks the salesman. Just what in hell does the boss want?

Even worse is the word *thing*. *Thing* means or fails to mean a million situations. The financial report becomes "the whole *thing*." "The *thing* is getting out of hand," says the boss to his secretary, meaning his wife has found out about their casual evenings together at the Schwartz Motel. "Get your *things* on," says the mother to her children. She wants them to dress. "A funny *thing* happened to me . . ."

Sleep

SLEEP is the one promise life makes us which it never reneges. Of all of life's pleasures, sleep undoubtedly is the one with the most undiminished joy, as valuable to us when we are infants as when we are septuagenarians. Sometimes, however, we are ashamed of this gift. The Puritan tradition in our society makes us feel guilty if we spend too much time in bed. The man who boasts that he never sleeps more than five hours a night believes he qualifies for some sort of special admiration. We have abolished the noonday nap which persists in calmer societies as a supremely civilized activity.

Sleep is there, it costs nothing, and we should take every advantage of it. We should never be ashamed of sleep. First of all it repairs the body and second, it keeps us out of mischief. Churchill and Sandburg manage to be in bed about ten hours a day. Churchill, in fact, gets two five-hour stretches of sleep a day. He retires at 5 P.M. and rises again at 10 P.M. Then he hits the hay again around 3 A.M. and no one sees him until around 1 o'clock in the afternoon. Sandburg says it doesn't really matter whether or not those hours are spent in sound sleep, the important thing is to lie in the bed, stretched out and at ease. The more time you spend in the bed, the less risk there is of losing your temper, and what is even more important, you will begin to appreciate the wonders of the everyday world.

TV commercials

I HAVEN'T joined in the game of blasting TV commercials. I remember when big city daily newspapers ran advertisements for brothels (massage parlors).

Since TV commercials, too, are entitled to "early days," they haven't been doing badly at all. But Heinz ketchup now advertises its product to the accompaniment of that wonderful hymn, "Land of Hope and Glory," from *Pomp and Circumstance*, by Elgar. This is just a little too much.

When I hear "Land of Hope and Glory," I think of Winston Churchill and Franklin D. Roosevelt signing the Atlantic Charter—without ketchup.

Hubcaps and marriage

In MID-TWENTIETH-CENTURY America there's a problem about hubcaps. I know some folks here in Charlotte who remove their automobile hubcaps Friday afternoon when they get home from work for the weekend. They are tired of having them stolen. Teen-agers steal these hubcaps and probably trade them for a few cents some place, or they do it for a thrill.

There's only one cure for this problem. Marriage. We have found that when the teen-ager marries, he stops stealing hubcaps. The psychologists who advise against early marriage have not taken this into consideration. Even if he marries at the age of sixteen, it ends his career as a hubcap stealer. There's something about marriage that gives a man a greater sense of responsibility and a more meaningful sense of direction. It is true he may go on to bigger things, but at least the hubcaps are safe.

The integrity of the post office

Nothing in this world has the integrity of a sealed envelope. A letter is compacted civilization. After my father emigrated to America, he still wrote home to his older brother and addressed his letter to: "Abraham Goldhirsch, who lives on the river Sereth, near Miculincz, Galicia, in the Austro-Hungarian Empire." It was always delivered.

If you want to find anyone in the world, the best bet is a letter posted to the last known address.

Uses of the newspaper

DURING the Depression of the 1930's newspapers had a greater utility than simply spreading the bad news of how much each stock had dropped. The folks, like myself, with holes in their shoes used to insulate their feet with folded newspapers. It works, too. My readers will have to take my word for it since holes in the shoe are phenomena unknown in these days of easy affluence. By far the best paper in New York for this purpose was the *Racing Form*. Nor was this because most of us bettors had holes in our shoes. The print in the *Racing Form* was finer and there was more of it and it lent this paper a wholly unsuspected substance.

The best thing to clean an auto's windshield is a newspaper because newsprint has a gentle abrasive action. In a pinch a newspaper can serve as an umbrella, although I recommend you read the paper first before venturing into the rain because you will not get to read it later.

But by far the supreme use the newspaper has in the American home relates to its use as a garbage pail liner and as garbage disposal sheets. No magazine, no glossy advertisement, throw-a-way pamphlet can make this claim.

Just how effectively newspapers perform varies from town to town. There are folks in Charlotte, North Carolina who wouldn't line their can with anything but the Charlotte *Observer* and there are others up in the Eastern suburbs who say nothing can compare with the Bridgeport *Post*. And for those who get rid of the coffee grounds via the garbage can instead of the sink, nothing beats the tabloids. The outsize paper, like the *Wall Street Journal*, does marvelously for apple peelings and peach skins but it is not so good for draining bacon. Nor should the *Wall Street Journal* or any financial page be used for lining drawers. You are much better off lining the bureaus with the sports pages or the theatre section. Whenever it is that you reline them, you have a printed relic of some interest. Stock averages are due to fluctuate and most certainly surprise you when you read them over five years later.

Apiarians tell me bees are magnetically attracted to sheet music. Why this should be remains a mystery. I have no intention of initiating an empirical study in depth. I know that fishmongers have always wrapped purchases in sheet music and it was at a fish store once that some of Johann Sebastian Bach's compositions were rescued by a discerning purchaser.

It might not be a bad idea for advertising agencies to boast of the home uses a paper has instead of repeating that mumbo jumbo about advertising linage increases and circulation gains.

It might be interesting for you, dear reader, to count up the ways in which you use your daily, and you could drop the managing editor a line about it and make him feel indeed he is serving society.

Immigrants and pioneers

WE JEWISH boys, immigrants and the sons of immigrants, could walk from Houston Street or Delancey Street or

Eldridge Street on the Lower East Side of New York to Washington Square Park and there board the open-air double-deck Fifth Avenue bus. Unhappily, the company long ago retired these buses. But, in my day, along about 1910, they ran constantly. For a dime we could go the length of Fifth Avenue into what was then the beginning of the Bronx. When the driver saw farmland, he turned around and went back.

Along the way, we passed places like Tiffany's and Black Starr & Frost jewelry stores whose pretty pins cost as much as our fathers made in a year. We passed the homes of the aristocracy—the Carnegies and the Vanderbilts—and the mansions of the rich Jews—Schiff, Warburg, and Pulitzer—immigrants who had made a success in America. They were men who wore not caps and caftans but opera capes and top hats. We went by the churches, Methodist, Presbyterian, Episcopalian, and Roman Catholic, and the famous Moorish-style Jewish Temple Emanu-El. At one point, if we stood on the seats, we could see the spires of Columbia University. Lucky students went to and fro, carrying huge armloads of books.

We took these bus rides to see the fine stores and the rich homes and the gleaming churches and the happy, absorbed students. We were passing through the open society. A dime was our passport.

We saw, from the top of that bus, in all its beauty, the promise America made.

And we could move from the Lower East Side if we chose, from the multilingual ghetto with its shouting peddlers and pungent smells, to other destinies, out past Grant's Tomb, right into the Bronx.

Nothing identifies America like the idea of mobility. It is one of the democratic ideals: it presupposes the individual's ability to move from class to class, from place to place, from one income level to another, and from one set of politics to a newer or an older set. There are no permanent stations in American life.

The reason for this fluid structure is that there are two traditions which distinguish us from all other nations. These are the Frontier Tradition and the Immigrant Tradition. For the first century of our life as a nation, we pushed against a western frontier that seemed ever expanding. Thousands rushed to it, to find gold, land, trade, or simply more room. The courage of these pioneers, their brusque and summary justice, their cruelty and hardness, still influence many of our attitudes even though some of us may be Americans one generation old who never had an adventure more exciting than a trip to the top of the Empire State Building.

At the same time these pioneers were pushing off, boatload after boatload of immigrants steamed from Europe. These immigrants left their homeland and sought a new life in what my mother always called *Die Goldene Medina* (The Golden Land). In Europe, the political and economic distinctions, the narrowing of ambition, the restrictions against free speech and religious freedom forced them out. Because they hated these conditions, they struck out in a strange land to face unnamed dangers. They succeeded for two reasons: they were courageous and wanted more than those who stayed at home; and native Americans helped them by establishing a free public school system which turned the immigrant class into a citizen class within a single generation.

Our immigrant and frontier traditions became related traditions. America is constantly absorbing the immigrant only to reproduce the pioneer. Not too long ago, a grandson of immigrants defined the New Frontier to us from the steps of the White House.

Thus, in many ways, we are a nation always on the move.

We say of ourselves we are a nation on wheels and this is true enough. Our national life is often described in the metaphors of "momentum," "impetus," "freewheeling," and our economy by "upturn," and "stocks advance."

More than the physical sensation of travel, we know what it is to be on the move in our very hearts. So in love with movement are we, that there are no longer compact groups among us. The Irish moved out of New York's "Hell's Kitchen" to Amsterdam Avenue, the Jews from the Lower East Side to Brooklyn and the Bronx, the Italians from Little Italy to Staten Island and Connecticut, and the Germans from Yorkville to Queens. And after a short digestive period, they were all on the move again, to the suburbs of Westchester, Long Island, and the Jersey coast.

Today no one can collect a family for a wedding or a funeral on a mere few hours' notice. One brother is in Waco, Texas, another in Madison, Wisconsin, and a married sister is in Los Angeles.

Because of our mobility we often bemoan our lack of roots. We might as well bemoan our breathing. It is in our nature to move about as it is in our nature to draw breath. In the last half-century, millions of Americans have traveled to every corner of the globe in three major wars. Countless other Americans have followed them to administer relief programs, to start new businesses, to man garrisons. In America, the average family will move once every four years.

Whether this is good or bad, I cannot say. I do say we must learn to live with it. We are all aboard that open-deck bus going along the Fifth Avenue of America and the world.

Strontium 90

THE level of strontium 90 is not very high. It is just a bit higher than last year, and that was just a little bit higher than the year before when there was barely enough to go round for everybody.

Go South, young man, go South

HEY, you all 20-to-25-year-olds, come South. Come South to the pioneer country. North Carolina may be your best bet, but rest assured your future will be just as bright in Georgia, South Carolina, Arkansas, Tennessee, Texas, or Virginia. Here is another frontier. We are looking at it nearly one hundred years after we thought the last one was closed.

The graduates of business administration schools, the technicians, the salesmen, the teachers, the manufacturers, the merchants, the distributors, the politically ambitious who journey South today may be unaware that the ghost of the Conestoga wagons and the trail blazers travel with them. For these new men are entering upon the urban-industrial frontier.

Even those manufacturers who come here to take advantage of what is laughingly called the "right to work" laws (which means cheap, non-union labor) will soon discover outside their factory doorstep the largest untapped consumer's market on the continent. This will be their bonus for coming South, the gratuity they are just discovering, the bonanza some already are exploiting.

This discovery explains the Southerner's frantic efforts to "save" free enterprise. The Southerner has only recently discovered free enterprise and it all seems just too good to be true. He is afraid someone will come along and take it away from him. The Southerner faces the same torment as the sourdough who made a strike and had to file a claim he worried someone might steal.

The cry of *states' rights* echoes this torment, this worry about whether he'll get to the government office to file his claim in safety. In actual fact, the South has been a federal preserve for the past thirty-five years, a preserve much like Yellowstone National Park, except the South is bigger and more complex. As late as 1946 there were a million people in my state who did not yet have electric lights. The Federal Government, through the REA, finally gave them electricity for the first time since Thomas A. Edison gave us the electric lamp in 1879.

The South moved into the industrial age when the Federal Government began subsidizing its agriculture, TVA, establishing the infantry, artillery, and air force training camps in the region, the missile sites, and the hundreds of millions of federal tax dollars which went into Southern airports, roads, hospitals, old-age pensions, veterans' benefits, welfare funds, laboratories, free school lunches, airspace industries, reclamation works, and oil-depletion allowances.

Traveling through the rural and mountain sections of the South lets one see the folks trooping to the mailbox for that brown envelope containing the Social Security, pension, or welfare check. It is a special treat to travel through Georgia, which now has the most up-to-date and most beautiful post offices of any state in the country. These spanking-new buildings occupy every obscure crossroad and they have been commissioned through the efforts of the two most vociferous *states' rights* champions in the country—Senators Richard Russell and Herman Talmadge.

This frontier will really floriate the day the Southerner gets the Negro off his back, the day when the white man goes about his own business unfettered by the worry of what the colored man is going to do next. When the white Southerner can throw off the shackles of the color line and stop worrying whether a fellow Southerner is amenable about moving to the back of the bus, he will be able to say to his boss: "Now looky here, you've been paying me 63¢ an hour less than you pay the fellow in New Jersey. He does the same job and works less hours. I never asked my fair share before because you told me you would keep the Negroes out of my schools, buses, restaurants, voting places, and swimming pools. But you can't. The Negro is in all of these places. So you better ante up that 63¢ an hour you owe me."

When racial segregation finally ends, the Southern gold rush will be on. The South will provide then the greatest urban-industrial growth in all history.

Come South, young man, come South. The climate is wonderful. The people are, in truth, hospitable. The schools are improving every semester. The opportunities for you and your children are better here than anywhere else. Take my advice. You will get all the aforementioned advantages plus the opportunity of getting rich.

Of all the things I've ever written, I am most positive of this truth: the South is the land of opportunity, the land of good fortune, the land of the future.